REVOLUTION IN MISSIONARY THINKING

REVOLUTION IN MISSIONARY THINKING

A Symposium

Edited by
William J. Richardson, M.M.

MARYKNOLL PUBLICATIONS
Maryknoll, New York
1966

Library of Congress Catalog Card Number: 66-27417

Nihil Obstat: Daniel V. Flynn, J.C.D.

Imprimatur: ✠ Terence J. Cooke, D.D., V.G.
Archdiocese of New York

June 22, 1966

Editor's Preface

Revolutions are not necessarily those of "national liberation" nor are they any longer to be considered the prerogative of Communists alone. Vatican II has set the wheels in motion for an international revolution within the previously "monolithic" Catholic Church. Just as political revolutions follow upon a radical change in ideology, so too is the updating within the Church dependent upon a new approach to many revered traditional institutions which have become sacred cows. Radically new concepts of the mission of the Church and its implementation are very much a part of this revolution.

A major hindrance to the international outreach of the Church is the concept that She must continue to expand the Kingdom of God in the same manner as Francis Xavier or Matteo Ricci during the golden ages of discovery and colonialism. Discovery is past and European colonialism is dead. In order to bring about the unbloody revolution in the hearts of men in all nations, we must begin with revolutionary ideas and ideals.

Today ideas are at a premium. Methods will follow from basic concepts and convictions. Re-evaluations are shaking our former confidence and self-assurance. This soul-searching is not good in itself, but shall be worth the anguish if it results in dynamic attitudes toward the Church's world-wide mission and the willingness to risk new ventures. The contributors to this symposium reflect many of these attitudes in their papers and jointly present an enthusiastic spirit of cooperation, courage, and openness in their views of the post-Vatican II age of missions.

The vehicle which gave expression to these ideas of a revolutionary mission within the Church was the annual meeting of the Mission Secretariat held in Washington, D.C., under the chairmanship of Father Frederick A. McGuire, C.M., executive secretary of the Secretariat. Publication of selected papers here is intended to provide an even wider audience for this necessary ideological base of future activity.

WM. J. RICHARDSON, M.M.
Maryknoll, New York

Table of Contents

Commentary from Abroad

MICHAEL C. PELLY, S.J.

There is an agonizing apostolic anguish in the Church today, felt with different intensities and expressed at different levels, to appraise the mystery of the Church "kept hidden" as St. Paul says, "from the beginning of time in the all-creating mind of God" (Eph. 3:9), and to assess our Christian response in terms of existential obligations. The annual meeting of the mission secretariat is testimony to such appraisal, as indeed was the Pro Mundi Vita Congress in Louvain in September 1964. Congresses like these "enlighten the prophetic consciousness of the Church, deepen our awareness of its mystery, and alert us to our individual and collective response to its needs."

Knowledge of the nature, the mission, and the destiny of the Church must precede any rational apostolic action. As Pope Paul VI phrases it, "The Church needs to reflect on Herself. She needs to feel the throb of Her own life. She must learn to know Herself better if She wishes to live Her own proper vocation and to offer to the world Her message of brotherhood and of salvation."[1]

[1] Paul VI, *Ecclesiam Suam*, N.C.W.C. edition, No. 25.

The Constitution on the Church clearly supplies us with "that better knowledge of Herself" which we need, in order to stir up that "fire on earth" which Christ our Lord came to enkindle. It is not a final or complete delineation of Her image, but it can supply us with a lifetime of fruitful meditation, and it may take generations to implement.

I would like to select two aspects of the revolutionary thinking which is crystallized for us in this dogmatic statement. The first is that it emphasizes the equality[2] of all the members of the people of God, antecedent to any functional differentiation between ministry and laity. This is new and vital and potentially explosive; it will cause much heart-searching within the Church, for it seems to set up a spiritual democracy within the monarchical framework of the people of God. Some of you may recall from your missionary experience, as Barbara Ward points out in her *The Rich and the Poor Nations,* that

> There was no concept of equality in traditional society. As one knows from still-existing tribal societies, leadership lies with the old men of the tribe. There is no way for the "young men" to claim equality. They simply have to wait for the years to pass. Seniority (as in the American Senate) also ensures that the leaders are men who respect the backward-looking traditions of the group and have a vested interest in the unequal prestige conferred by advancing years. It is the inescapable recipe for extreme conservatism.[3]

[2] Constitution on the Church, N.C.W.C. edition, No. 32. This document is hereafter referred to in the body of the text as *De Ecclesia.*
[3] Barbara Ward, *The Rich Nations and the Poor Nations* (New York, Norton, 1962), p. 45.

Our political and social history for the past two hundred years bears adequate testimony to the justice of this remark.

THE PEOPLE OF GOD

The first two great chapters of the Constitution, taken in conjunction with the fourth, are an inspiring exposition of Christian status. They correct a weakness of our recent ecclesiology, which emphasized too much the status of the hierarchy at the expense of the whole people of God. They dissolve the institutional dichotomy between teachers and taught, between the so-called active and passive elements in the Church. As Father Bell so aptly quoted, there is a decentration away from the hierarchical office so that the center of all ecclesial life is not the hierarchy, but the people of God. We are all servants of God, but some of us are more servants than others, since we are chosen and committed to ministry. Indeed in a certain sense these magnificent chapters reverse polarity in emphasizing the apostolic role of the layman and thus releasing an enormous lay potential. One has only to appreciate the tremendous lay contribution to the mission activity of other Christian churches, to realize how much our own lay potential lies latent and dormant.

The laity share the priestly and prophetic character of Christ. They, and not the clergy, have the chief duty to transform secular society, and both parties must recognize and respect each other's roles. The clergy may counsel, stimulate, inspire, advise, but it is the responsibility of the layman, and not the priest, nor the religious, to take and to implement decisions. Nor are laymen merely instruments of policy. In the whole multifarious activity of human society, they are the policy makers. Indeed, antecedent to this tremendous Constitution on the Church, antecedent even to the Ten Commandments, they were given in Adam a command to "increase and multiply and fill the earth and make it yours" (Gen. 1:28); they were given dominion over things, a dominion which has never been revoked. The Constitution clarifies their role as consecrators of the temporal order, as those who are especially called and, therefore, have a vocation in the strict sense, to renew all things in Christ.

To renew men is the office of the clergy, by our ministry of service. And if we are to execute this office properly, if we are not to be "blind guides leading the blind," we must be thoroughly aware of the existential human problems of the laity, taking the stature of maturity in a rapidly changing world, a revolutionary world, as Father Burke so justly pointed out. And so with diverse roles; the clergy must actively cooperate with the laity, for the laity's priestly function is to mediate, not only to receive from the Church and to give to the world, but also to receive from the world and to give to the Church. The Constitution is not merely a charter of the laity; it amounts to a mobilization formula for a missionary Church. The Church as a community of believers is always in mission to those who do not believe, through a ceaseless and universal preaching, "in season and out of season," from which no Church member is exempt. This is the prophetic role of the laity.

I stress this revolutionary mission thinking with regard to the laity, first, because I think it cannot be overstressed; secondly, because the catastrophic drop in priestly and religious vocations over the past ten years is a world-wide phenomenon, highlighting an enormous need for the laity to help in evangelizing a rapidly expanding world. And thirdly, because it puts into a better perspective the second aspect I wish to speak about, collegiality, which may have been overemphasized in our minds through too much polemic and publicity.

COLLEGIALITY

We all owe a special debt of gratitude to Father Burke for his magnificent exposition of this subject. I would like to add these reflections. Collegiality redresses an ecclesiological weakness left over since Vatican I, the tendency to overstress the papacy at the expense of the episcopacy. The hierarchy is seen as an instrument of service within the Church; the authority of the bishops, collective, and by divine right preceding their individual authority, so that by divine right their responsibility for the whole Church precedes their individual responsibility for the local diocese. The authority of the Church is thus essentially and initially unified. The bishops share one authority, but this unified, collective authority derives from, flows from, is the direct responsibility for universal mission placed on the Apostles as a group and transmitted through them to the historical hierarchy. This has been very clearly demonstrated by Father Burke in his exegesis.

And this, if you develop the thought, is of supreme importance. First, that authority within the Church is *collective;* secondly, it is, for want of a better word, *commissioned.* As a collective authority to teach, sanctify, and govern the whole people of God, the normal authority of the espiscopate is exercised in communion with and presided over by the pope. The authority of the individual bishop is participation in the one collective apostolic authority and, as such, is controlled and limited by the authority of the college taken collectively, and of its head.

> This power which they personally exercise . . . is ultimately regulated by the supreme authority of the Church, and can be circumscribed by certain limits, for the advantage of the Church or of the faithful (*De Ecclesia,* No. 27).

This seems to mean that a check and balance system of control has been introduced into the power corridors within the Church. No single bishop, nor any group of bishops, can arbitrarily act on their own, against the common good of the Church. Singly and collectively, they are not merely accountable to God, as stewards of the mysteries that God has committed to them; they are accountable also to the one, collective, apostolic authority concerned with the common purposes of the Church.

> Bishops, as vicars and ambassadors of Christ, govern the particular Churches entrusted to them, by their counsel, exhortation, example, and even by their authority and sacred power, which indeed they use

> only for the edification of their flock in truth and holiness, remembering that he who is greater should become as the lesser and he who is the chief become as the servant (*De Ecclesia,* No. 27).

The order of words is significant. They "govern . . . by their counsel, exhortation, example, and even by their authority and sacred power." The word order is significant, surely, of the primacy of the ministry of service over the exercise of authority and sacred power. Indeed, authority in lawmaking or power in law enforcement are circumscribed by the apostolic purpose of the edification of the flock in truth and holiness—confined, therefore, to the spheres of worship and revealed truth together with its theological conclusions. The use of a bishop's authority and sacred power in other fields is not just limited but excluded. If they speak in other areas of truth, they speak only with the authority which their professional competence in these areas gives them. And, like any other professional, they have no power to compel assent. Thus the evangelical concept of the freedom of the sons of God is perfectly reconcilable with this restored evangelical concept of the authority and power possessed by the bishop. A vital distinction is thus made between the permanent divine structure of authority and power, and the historical structures which developed through civil, social, or political exigency, or by Providential disposition. This distinction is important for harmonious dialogue between bishops and major superiors.

Since episcopal authority and sacred power are strictly confined, there arises the problem: of what kind is the authority necessarily required for Church administration or government, and how are we to reconcile our concept of its historical exercise in institutional forms with the new ecclesiology of a ministry of service? The Constitution on the Church seems to imply that the one collective authority, insofar as it is related to government, strictly so-called, or administration, is a commissioned authority—flowing from the mission given to the Apostles and thus to the bishops. As such it would be analogous to commissioned authority in the army or in business or organizational life—an authority that is rooted in executive responsibility to perform a precise function or to accomplish a specific purpose. To understand the conceptual revolution which this involves, may I quote from *Administration and Social Ethics* by Father William Ferree, S.M.:

> Responsibility is the duty to perform a delegated function; authority is the right to make and enforce decisions within the delegated limits. The popular conception of authority and obedience places them in two different kinds of people, known as superiors and inferiors. Administrative theory finds it much more useful to consider the two as they always coexist in the same person. The popular view considers authority as being primary, and obedience as being a secondary and dependent function. In the administrative view, it is obedience or executive responsibility, which is primary, as being close to the purposes, and authority is a "result" of such an executive responsibility.
>
> Thus authority and responsibility are not two quite different qualities which exist in different kinds of

> persons, superiors and inferiors; but they are correlative properties which always co-exist in the same person whether he be superior or inferior. The only difference between superior and inferior is their hierarchical grade: the structure of authority and responsibility is exactly the same in both. A great deal of administrative romanticism and human suffering could be removed from the world if these fundamental relationships could become better understood.[4]

Perhaps, in the understanding of these relationships, there lies the solution to the crisis of obedience and authority within the Church.

Collegiality also provides an in-built pragmatic principle for achieving unity within the Church. Collective responsibility issuing in collective action in the top echelon of the Church can only be achieved by a real meeting of minds and hearts, an effective dialogue with each other and with the Church, and with the world, making it the effective sign of inner unity in love, which Christ intended for this sacrament which is the Church He created (*cf. De Ecclesia*, No. 1). In setting up the principle of cooperation among the bishops and, by implication, of exhortation and example at all levels, collegiality challenges the geographical and sociological isolation of the hierarchy and the individualism which has fragmented apostolic action. It enormously strengthens the ecclesiastical pyramid at the top level and lays open the way for a new Church administration concerned with purposes, achieved by lateral as well as vertical communications.

[4] William Ferree, S.M., *Administration and Social Ethics* (Fribourg, 1962), pp. 108, 109.

In setting up a new polarity for the missionary bodies and the mission-sending societies, away from Rome and toward control by regional or local hierarchies, collegiality presents us with the special problem of the theological meaning of the missionary bodies. Pro Mundi Vita will conduct a study of this matter later on.

OUR RESPONSE TO DE ECCLESIA

Re-education: The problem of the Church is to make this vast program of the Constitution viable by individual as well as collective action. The first obvious individual response is to read, meditate, and try to understand this magnificent document. You are the leaders, the teachers, the mediators between God and man, and between God and things. It would be tragic if we were deficient in our individual responsibility not merely toward ourselves, but toward those who depend upon us. There is a psychological exigency in human nature to first formulate an idea before acting upon it. None of us is exempt from the labor which this involves, if we are adequately to fulfill our ministry of service.

Secondly, we need to mount a massive re-education and re-formation program, to the Church as mission, to the new approach, to collective as well as individual responsibility. This program should permeate all levels from grade school through university, seminary, and religious training. Prescinding from priorities here, I would add a plea for the development of an intellectual elite, not merely among missionaries but particularly among the laity. Theirs will be the chief burden of the dialogue with contemporary society, and they must be saturated with a Catholic culture, which can speak clearly and meaningfully to the cultural leaders of Asian societies. The need is equally valid for Africa and Latin America. Pope Pius XII, in his *Fidei Donum,* had the courage to call for an intellectual elite from an embryonic African church. The political and social influence of the Latin American universities is extraordinary and there is a crying need there for an apostolate of intelligence. The Catholic colleges and universities in the United States constitute the one extensive system of higher education in the Catholic world. Perhaps they are too much geared to the production of professional careers, and altogether too little to international Catholic voluntary service overseas.

Bishops everywhere are becoming aware of both the dangers and the potentialities of the social media communications. Would it be too much to hope that the American bishops will give a lead to the rapidly growing English-speaking Catholic world by setting up a Catholic communications center with coordinated radio and television services?

In the sphere of journalism, the missionary bodies and mission-sending societies are in many places deploring the various forms of wastage, the fragmentation and the image of their work projected by their mission magazines. You may already know that the Germans, with characteristic thoroughness, have solved the problem in their own way. As of February 1965, the missionary societies have been combining their resources to produce a common national missionary magazine, worthy of the Church in Germany and of the cause they serve, while catering through distribution inserts for the diverse interests of the missionary bodies. This solution may profitably be adopted in other places. Personally, I believe that missionaries in training at home, and missionaries in the field, need a technical journal designed especially for them. An editorial board of expert journalists, missiologists, anthropologists, mission economists, and so forth, could edit a journal somewhat like Concilium, in which they would collect, collate, and translate, in digest form, the world output of all thought relevant to mission as well as to developing mission trends.

But the main burden of this massive re-formation and re-education program, at the grass-roots level, will fall obviously on all educators, upon the priests, the Brothers, the nuns, the laity, who teach in grade schools, high schools, colleges, and universities, upon those involved in Sister formation, upon the faculties in seminaries and houses of religious formation. A thorough re-evaluation of educational goals, method, and structures is called for, at all levels. This re-evaluation should distinguish clearly between the permanent divine structure of the Church and the institutional forms which historical necessity or divine providence brought into being to serve concrete needs, which either no longer exist, or, if they do, could be supplied by a trained laity, thus releasing priests and religious for their proper work of evangelization. This re-evaluation should take a long look at the enormous field of lay responsibility for the consecration of the temporal order. In all the fields of purely human endeavor, in the family, in work, in the professions, in education, indeed, in all social and political life, the laity have the right, not merely to be consulted but the duty *to decide, to make the policy,* and this by God's command antecedent to any Constitution on the Church. It is the duty of the ministry of service to provide the laity with a theology of the family, a theology of work, a theology of education, a theology for the social and political order. Ours it is to stimulate, to counsel, to inspire, and above all to encourage. This re-evaluation will benefit enormously by the sharing of knowledge and techniques acquired at national or regional levels and distributed through international Church structures.

In this matter of cooperation, we might well pay closer attention to the words of Pope Pius XII in his very first encyclical, *Summi Pontificatus:*

> The accomplishment of the task of regeneration by adapting Her means to the altered conditions of the times and the new needs of the human race, is an essential and maternal office of the Church. Committed to Her by Her Divine Founder, the preaching of the Gospel, by which are inculcated to men truth, justice, and charity, and the endeavor to implant its precepts solidly in mind and conscience, is the most noble and fruitful work for peace. That mission would seem as if it ought to discourage by its very grandeur the hearts of those whose who make up the Church militant. But *that cooperation in the spread of the Kingdom of God* [our italics] which in every century is effected in different ways, with varying instruments, with manifold hard struggles, is a command incum-

> bent on everyone who has been snatched by divine grace from the slavery of Satan and called in Baptism to citizenship of the Kingdom of God.[5]

It is a curious comment on communications in the Church that twenty-seven years after these words were written, we should have reached only the talking stage about the need for cooperation in missionary endeavor.

I think it is vital that we should radically change the pattern of our pedagogic methods. Our educational system tends to foster an unhealthy individualism, developing competition and a climate of conflict in the commercial, professional, and social spheres. We need to form a social sense, to form a corporate Catholic social conscience, not just to pay it lip service in textbooks. We have to foster the sense of interdependence on each other, of awareness and concern for the neighbor in need, whether at home or abroad. I do not think that this is possible without a revolutionary revision of our methods. Group consciousness has to be formed by living it, not just by talking about it. Hence in all schools and at all levels, the techniques of group listening, of groups studying together, of groups working and acting together, must be structured into our secular education as well as into our seminaries and houses of religious formation.

I believe that the decadence of the affluent society, documented so dramatically by Fellini in *La Dolce Vita,* is fundamentally social boredom—the malaise of the uncommitted. Youth all over the world is crying out for committal, for commital to sacrifice, for committal

[5] Pius XII, *Summi Pontificatus,* N.C.W.C. edition, p. 34.

to an in-built, inherent idealism, and for committal in groups. This has been magnificently demonstrated in America by the Peace Corps. Here is the psychological basis for vocations in the widest sense; the vocational crisis may well be due to our inept methods in challenging youth. Let us put an end to educational babying and educate toward maturity, toward the making of rational, responsible, convinced citizens of the Kingdom of God, not merely in our secular education, but most of all in our religious and priestly formation.

Furthermore, there is an enormous unreaped harvest of lay vocations in the field of adult education. Interested enquirers might study with profit the lay-directed Pauline Association in Sydney, Australia. They have a three-prong program. First, adult education proper, with a theological basis but ranging over family problems, marriage and career counselling, labor relations, politics, economics, and current affairs, with a periodical produced by coordinated teams of experts in all fields. Secondly, lest theory should evaporate in a vacuum, it mounts practical group projects in the social apostolate and, thirdly, gives orientation training to lay volunteers for overseas service in New Guinea, Papua, and Indonesia.

Specialization: Accompanying and, perhaps, dictating the trends, modes, methods, and pace of the grass-roots re-education program, there must be a missionary specialization, and that in specific fields.

First, in *mission research,* clarifying purposes, evaluating means, using the precise projections of statistical data to forecast likely trends in rapidly changing social structures. We will need the delineation of the *now* in the pattern of future responsibilities. I would make a special plea for wholehearted support for CARA (Center for Applied Research in the Apostolate), which is admirably structured toward the end for which it was designed. In this field, as in so many others, we might make our own the terse direction of Thomas Alva Edison to his research workers: "There's a better way; find it!"

Second, we need everywhere *pastoral institutes,* internationally linked together under the new structure proposed in the Decree on the Church's Missionary Activity and directed by the Bishops' Conference, the Conference of Major Superiors, and responsible leaders of the main lay organizations. These must be the heart of the new apostolate in the Church, surveying existential situations, assessing pastoral priorities according to the criteria of urgency, importance, and directives from the top, and making short- and long-term plans. The hierarchies of Africa are far ahead of those of the white West in these matters. But to delay pastoral planning is dangerous, if we wish to avoid disheartening and discouraging dedicated priests, religious, and laity, who deserve the best. The Pro Mundi Vita studies on vocations are a warning that, perhaps within twenty years, Europe will be able to supply only half the personnel available today.

Third, a survey of most national mission statistics reveals a pattern of haphazard, uncontrollable, and therefore ineffective performance, lacking *home centers of specialized orientation studies,* linked to similar *re-orientation training centers* on a continental level for the developing churches, not merely for expatriate clergy and religious and laity, but also for indigenous clergy, who when sent to Rome are usually Westernized.

Last, there is a wide field for *lay action by specialists* in all countries in providing hospitality to overseas students. This apostolate was given to national hierarchies by Pius XII in *Fidei Donum*. In some places, the apostolate has gone by default.

Communications: Besides the clarification of purposes through scientific research, and the proper planning of priorities in a missionary Church, shaped in a true strategy, and the tactical deployment of personnel and other resources, there is a crying need for structural coordination for what are called communications. Purposes, plans, and priorities can be known only insofar as they are communicable. This is the business of administration. An up-dated Church administration is urgently required at all levels.

It is particularly vital for religious. Since they donate themselves completely, they deserve it. They are not expendable. Disillusioned subjects of an inept autocratic authority either give up trying, or bury themselves in a frenetic activity, building, organizing, administering, collecting money, to the detriment of better pastoral activity. This is a deep malaise in the Church, a wasted potential. It can be a dangerous scandal, tarnishing Her image in the secular world.

We have much to learn from the vast literature on administration techniques coming off American printing presses, and indeed, already analyzed by Father

William Ferree, S.M., with a view to application in Church government.[6]

Dialogue within the Church: Finally, none of this will be possible without permanent, frank, and open discussion at all levels within the Church. Dialogue is the fashionable word, but this is really an apostolate, examined in all its aspects by Pope Paul in his *Ecclesiam Suam,* which should be "must" reading for all bishops and superiors, and indeed for everyone "called to citizenship in the Kingdom of God."

CONCLUSION

Europe has borne the chief burden of the developing churches down the centuries. The United States is really only beginning. Less than three weeks ago, I was touring Europe's most sophisticated social structure in Flemish Limbourg, when my eye was attracted to a large advertisement, which read thus, "Visit the Nuts Museum in Bastogne!"

Europe remembers Americans for their courage, candour, and generosity. And Europe trusts that in the not too distant future the Holy Spirit will quicken the American special gift of technique to mobilize, plan, and deploy her compact, vast resources to put new life into the rapidly developing churches of the world.

[6] William Ferree, S.M., *op. cit.*

Collegial Responsibility for the Needy Churches

Eugene Burke, C.S.P.

> The Church, "like a stranger in a foreign land, presses forward amid the persecutions of the world and the consolations of God," announcing the cross and the death of Christ until He comes. By the power of the risen Lord it is given strength that it might, in patience and in love, overcome its sorrows and its challenges, both within itself and from without, and that it might reveal to the world, faithfully though darkly, the mystery of its Lord until, in the end, it will be manifested in full light (*De Ecclesia*, No. 8).

By these words the Fathers of the Second Vatican Council give a primary emphasis to the fact that the pilgrim Church, the people of God, is involved in the historical process and so as a community of living men and women acts in history and interacts with history. It is thereby a community in which the risen Lord speaks here and now, calling upon His members to meet challenges from within and from without. In fact, it is the actualities of history and its human developments that are the very source of these challenges, these questions, to which the pilgrim Church must respond if it would reveal the mystery of its Lord. However mighty the acts of God, the advance of His kingdom has always involved free cooperation, free response, free commitment. Only if the people of God willingly listen to the Spirit can the Church reveal the mystery of God as it should.

Yet, if the challenges of this our day are to be responded to; if faithful to our calling we are to make manifest Christ and His Gospel in our own time, it can only be through the Spirit of God. For it is the Spirit of God who enables us to understand the deep things of God revealed in His Son. For what the Constitution on the Church makes strikingly evident is that authentic pastoral concerns and all truly pastoral action flow from and are an essential dimension of God's revelation in Christ. The more deeply we understand the doctrines we assent to by Christian faith, the more urgently pastoral become the consequences of what we believe. For Christian doctrine is not a formula but a living idea with a depth and richness that is more clearly expressed and taught the longer it lasts.[1] Because it is a living, vital reality, it has "aspects many and bearings many, mutually connected and growing one out of another, and all parts of a whole, with a sympathy and a correspondence keeping pace with the ever-changing necessities of the world, multiform, prolific, and ever resourceful,"[2] and it is this necessary relation between dogma and pastoral office, between revelation more deeply understood and so developing a response to the challenge of our age, which has deter-

[1] *Cf.* John Henry Newman, *Essay on the Development of Christian Doctrine* (New York, Longmans, Green, 1897), p. 56.
[2] *Ibid.*

mined the shape of this chapter on collegial responsibility and the needy churches.

The very understanding of the depth and the extent of the challenge offered here is underlined by the choice of the term "needy churches" rather than say missionary churches. This usage looks to emphasizing two things. First that it is the Church as a whole that is the mission, and that its every member is charged with the missionary mandate wherever the Church is actualized. Secondly, it is clear that the older conception of mission churches, missionary churches, church missions, simply does not take into account the actual situation or express properly the nature of the Church itself. The vision of the missionary apostolate as a kind of spiritual crusade in which whole peoples and nations were converted to the Church, while understandable and in many instances feasible in another age, is now no longer viable. At best, it was a fact of cultural history and sociological development rather than theology. It failed, too, to take into full account the eschatological goal of the Church as the Light of the Gentiles and so came frequently to be identified with what today is called colonialism.

Today, however, any consideration of mission must begin by endeavoring to understand the transformation of the world in which we live. For underlying all the clashes and threats, the "brushfire wars," revolutions, and the threats of nuclear warfare, has been the inexorable diffusion of the technological revolution and its effects. It is a revolution which, in our time, is now beginning to revolutionize man himself, offering him an increasing potentiality for mastering his environment and his history. This is clearly discerned in the realm of communications, mass media of entertainment and information, as well as in international organizations such as the United Nations and its many instrumentalities for health, labor, children, education, and peace. It seems to me, too, that it is both dramatically and effectively symbolized in such efforts as the Peace Corps.

Yet underlying these obvious manifestations is a more profound reality, the growing affirmations of certain common human values that concern man's dignity and freedom. These affirmations are sometimes fully matured, sometimes ill-conceived, sometimes erratically and even childishly expressed. But they are there and no Christian mission dare ignore or deny them. And it is the search to implement these values that has given rise to two developments which confront the Christian mission even to the point of hostility.

SOCIALIZATION

The first of these is socialization. This is not to be confused with collectivism either political or social. As used in modern terminology, it means: "the general movement of the human race fulfilling its potentialities by means of corporate organizations such as family movements, distributive groups, institutions and the state." Of course, such a movement can be made to serve ends destructive of the human personality, yet as Pope John has pointed out in both *Mater et Magistra* and *Pacem in Terris,* such socialization also offers unparalleled opportunity for truly human living. For health, education, economic opportunity become corporate and public responsibilities and so open possibilities of personal life and cultural existence unthinkable even thirty years ago.

NATIONALISM

The other manifestation of the effort to concretize human values would seem to me to be nationalism. From the point of view of mission, this can be looked on as simply an extreme reaction to colonialism and paternalism that is temporary and will ultimately moderate. This may be possible, but I believe it is dangerous to be satisfied with this diagnosis. For this new nationalism stands as a real enemy to the whole Christian mission as conceived of in terms of the nineteenth-century Christian expansion—an expansion so often implicated with the thesis of the white man's burden. This new nationalism may have deep emotional roots; it may have political motivations; it may be juggled by politicians, grasping for power; it may be unjust to and destructive of the Christian missionary contribution. Yet, I am convinced, it represents a movement that is essentially legitimate and necessary, for it means an all-out effort of these needy nations to stand on their own feet. It unites peoples who have been thrust to the ground by poverty and colonization and, all too often, exploitation both foreign and domestic. It bespeaks an effort to give form to human values in their own cultural perspectives. Hence, they seek to incarnate these human values into their own cultural developments in terms of family and leisure and old age. Whether it be in the newly independent nations of Africa or the age-old cultures of Asia, nationalism is a factor that begets cohesion and power to confront what they see as threatening their opportunity to stand on their own feet. To ignore this is to invite disaster for any future Christian mission. Yet, these are the nations and the people in which the needy churches must labor and develop and be the sign of Christ's saving words.

For the believing Christian, however, this whole modern movement toward unity and common values has a profound and far-reaching theological dimension. We believe that man's choice for and movement toward unity has its actual source in God's own saving design. The Christian faith at its very heart affirms that this call to be one with all men is a call to be one with Christ and through Christ. Faith further attests that this call to unity is historically anterior to man's own choice. Radically, therefore, every human being is really related to the Church, since the call to be gathered together in the people of God is addressed to every human being through the very fact of the Incarnation. So God's self-giving to all humanity is a factual dimension of human history. Hence, as Father Schillebeeckx notes, this factual aspect is an explicit epiphany, historically and humanly visible. It is God's mercy and love for all men revealing itself in and through the Church and the Church bearing witness to it. "Thanks therefore to Christ's historical coming, there is in living humanity a kind of built-in compass pointing to the Church. Her missionary activity is merely the counterpart of this. This pointing to the Church, or mankind's need of Her in the concrete, and, on the other hand,

Her going out to mankind, are both visible forms of the one operative salvation which our Lord is in the Spirit of God, *Pneuma Theou*. In both, Jesus the Christ visits His messianic community that He acquired upon the cross to prepare for Himself His eschatological bride without spot unto the glory of God the Father." [3]

Up to this point, I have been working to set up what seems to me the necessary context for any fruitful discussion of collegial responsibility for the needy churches. The amount of space devoted to this is due to my personal conviction that there is no pastoral activity worthy of the name that does not have as its primary source the theological implications of what we believe. Correlatively, however, pastoral activity must be directed to and attuned to and able to react vitally with the actual situation of its time. Thus, we have seen the modern movement toward the unity of mankind under the impetus of the technological revolution. We have also noted the spiritual dimension of this movement in the increasing awareness of common human values. Attention has been called to the efforts to concretize these values through socialization and nationalism. Yet this historical moment has an inescapable theological dimension by reason of the Incarnation, for it is in the light of and by reason of the Incarnation we believe that the Church is the visible epiphany of God's saving gift, the revelation of the mystery of the Lord which all humanity needs and which must reach out to all humanity. Hence the

[3] Edward Schillebeeckx, O.P., "The Church and Mankind," in *The Church and Mankind*, Concilium, Vol. I (Glen Rock, N.J., Paulist Press, 1965), p. 89.

Church "is not simply the exclusive group of those who are saved but the communion of those who are called to live in the service of the many—a sign raised among the nations." It is the interaction of these three truths—the Church as the visible sign of God's grace for all mankind—that constitutes the context for collegial responsibility for the needy churches.

COLLEGIALITY

It is true, of course, that it is the whole people of God that is set aside and consecrated for the service of God. It is also true that it is the living community as a totality that prolongs and extends the mission of Christ in the world. Yet it is also true that this missionary mandate is given in a special way to the hierarchy. As the successors of the Apostles gathered around Peter, they have the direct collegial responsibility to evoke, stimulate, and sustain the apostolic mission of the Church. It falls directly on them by divine institution to be at once the witnesses par excellence of the unity and catholicity of Christ's Church. At the same time, theirs is the responsibility for making each member of the Church aware of his mission responsibility for the whole of humanity called to God through Christ.

To appreciate the full significance of this double responsibility, however, we must return to the doctrinal roots of collegiality itself. For modern exegesis distinguishes two stages in the New Testament development of the apostolic college. The first stage is the choice of *the Twelve* by Christ. In this first stage, the Twelve represent a directly eschatological symbol of the fulfillment of God's promises. Israel had expected that its final restoration would bring about the restoration of its original twelve tribes—a sign of its cosmic fullness. So Christ in choosing the Twelve proclaims that these are the last days; the messianic era has begun and Israel is gathered together in spiritual fullness as God has promised. It is after Pentecost that this perspective is enlarged to incorporate the notion of witness to the risen Christ. From this point on, it is the apostolate that is in the foreground, but the significance of the Twelve is not lost and continued to be used to interpret the apostolic office as manifesting God's promises to the new Israel. For the office of the Twelve, first of all, signifies the new covenant fulfilled in a new people gathered together by faith and not by race. The sign that they are gathered together by the redemptive resurrection is the Twelve whom Christ has chosen and who bear witness to Him and His risen life. The symbolism thus has meaning only in terms of the group centering on the Rock. Hence, each individual member has significance only in and through the group.

Modern theology drawing on this exegetical background, as well as patristic thought, emphasizes the very same point in its presentation of collegiality. Christ formed the Apostles after the manner of a college and the bishops by divine institution have succeeded to the place of the Apostles. Hence they constitute an apostolic college together with Peter. In the light of this, it seems clear that the individual bishop is not a successor of an individual apostle. It is because he belongs to the college—the universal episcopate—that he is a successor of the Apostles. It is, therefore, the apostolic college that holds the fullness of authority over the whole Church. Each member of the college, like the Apostles, is directly responsible to Peter, precisely because he and his successors are the divinely instituted heads of the college. Thus each of the Apostles and their successors have a direct personal function with regard to the Church as a whole. Hence the Church is not and cannot be simply an aggregation of individual churches or administrative elements. Rather, it is one Church, one body, one people because the original reality, the apostolic college, is called into being as an inseparable unity. The Church is one because the apostolic college, the universal episcopate united with the pope, is one.

This skeletal outline of the theology of collegiality should not obscure its flesh and blood reality, nor should it leave it as a purely juridical formulation. For collegiality, in scriptural terms, is the supreme symbol of that brotherhood whereby, through Baptism, all Christians are brothers of the First-born of the Father. For it is the fraternal communion of the bishops with one another and with Peter that constitutes the unity of the universal Church. Each local church is a realization and a manifestation of the fullness of the Church of Christ. But the whole Church, one and Catholic, exists by reason of the collegiality of the successors of the Apostles. So unity, apostolicity, catholicity derive from collegiality. Collegiality, however, derives from the communion of bishops which is the work of the Spirit of God—the soul of the Church.

From this follows another consequence undergirding all charismata proper to the episcopacy. The collegial responsibility symbolizes the very nature of the living Church in a way no other ecclesial element can. For the Church is above all a community of love and service, a love and a service which are the work of the Spirit of Christ. For whoever is moved by the Spirit is moved by the very love that Christ gives unceasingly to His Church to nourish it. It is this love that St. Paul saw as the supreme reality in the Church, as well as in the Christian life, and which enables every Christian to live and proclaim the Gospel. It is this same love that creates the unity and catholicity of the Church and which makes the office of bishop the most evident symbol of the Good Shepherd's love for His sheep. It is for this reason that the office of bishop, collegially formed to serve the whole people of God, demands by its very nature a love of the whole Church, a readiness, a willingness, a sense of obligation to serve the whole Church, all the churches, to the best of his ability and opportunity. For he is a successor of the Apostles because, first, he is incorporated in the universal episcopate by his consecration. In the words of Pius XII: "But if every bishop is the proper pastor only of that portion of the flock entrusted to his care, his quality as a legitimate successor of the Apostles by divine institution renders him jointly responsible for the apostolic mission of the Church." [4]

Logically, also, a fully exercised collegial responsibility would demand that the bishop bear witness to the universal Church in the local church whose shepherd he is. All that touches on the good or the needs or the problems of the universal Church—the *Catholica*—should find voice and symbol in him. The sense

[4] Pius XII, *Fidei Donum*, Propagation of the Faith edition, p. 12.

of catholicity whereby the charity of Christ reaches out to all humanity must be made evident through his teaching office and its many channels. To allow chauvinism or provincialism or parochialism to block out the Catholic vision of his flock is to fail in his obligation to the universal Church. Since he is teacher, apostolic witness, pastor, and high priest, the local church of God, of which he is father and spouse, should be as vitally and lovingly united to the whole Church as he is by the very nature of his episcopal office.

RE-EDUCATION FOR MISSION

The application of these theological perspectives on collegiality to the problem of the needy churches can be done on many levels. For the purposes of this chapter, I should like to select some of the most general so as to best illustrate my main theses. The first of these concerns the exercise of the collegial responsibility in the local church itself. Confining myself only to the United States and evaluating the actual situation, I feel that a far-reaching effort at re-education on the Church as mission is required. By far, the majority of our adult Catholics have been formed in terms of the missionary ideas coming out of the nineteenth century and going up to World War I. The global, sociological character of the mission, the need for an understanding of cultural and social anthropology in forming the missionary of today is understood by a very small minority. The far-reaching consequences of technology, socialization, nationalism from the perspective of Christian mission are rarely depicted outside of technical journals. The need to develop a non-Western Christianity that will truly serve as a meeting place with Jesus Christ for whole areas of the human race that are non-Western by tradition and frequently by hostile conviction is a totally unknown horizon for most American Catholics. Needed to be developed on a major scale is the conviction that being a Catholic requires personal partici-pation in the missionary activity of the Church and this is not resolved by the vicarious method of collections. By and large, we are aware of the enormity of the mission problem in South America and how rapidly the situation is deteriorating. The news reports have made all too evident the destruction wrought on the African mission enterprise in the Congo and in other countries. Clear, too, is the virtual destruction of what was, perhaps, the most intensive Christian mission effort of modern times—China. Yet to what extent have the reasons for these failures been fully evaluated and the conclusions honestly discussed and debated for our re-education? How well developed and understood are the lessons learned here, and how well are they being communicated? Other things might be noted, but the ones indicated show something of the task that must be undertaken in each local church if mission education is going to arouse the large-scale response the times demand. In the words of Pius XII: "This [apostolic] fervor directs itself toward the de-Christianized regions of Europe and the vast territories of South America. . . . It has pity for the spiritual poverty of the innumerable victims of modern atheism, above all for the young who grow in ignorance and sometimes in their hatred for God. All are necessary and urgent tasks which require from everyone a reawakening of apostolic energy, creating 'great legions of apostles similar to those which the Church knew at Her dawn.'"[5]

This need for mission re-education of the faithful carries with it an inescapable implication. If it is to come about, then those who are the primary collaborators in the bishop's teaching office must also be deeply and fully formed in this new and urgently demanded mission approach. The priests and religious communities, who serve the pulpit and the classrooms and by a thousand paths work to form the people of God, must have open to them the world of missiology as it now is. Any deeply conscious sense of mission requires educational formation, and in depth, if it is to be fruitful and effective. In the seminary there is needed a missiology course that is not simply a history of the Christian missions, but a genuine theology of mission for the world today. Such a theology would give full import to the cultural and sociological and political factors that must be understood. Out of this we will come to the realization that home and foreign missions in our modern world are complementary and interdependent. In short, a theological development of the true idea of mission as "that spiritual activity which, originating in the Trinitarian processes, consists in preaching the Gospel to non-Christians and in establishing among them in an indigenous and stable fashion the entire Christian economy for the sake of their own salvation, the full devel-

[5] *Ibid.*, pp. 2-3.

opment of the Mystical Body, and the glory of the Father through the Son in the Spirit." [6]

On the national level, there seems to me a very obvious possible development. For, as the National Conference of Bishops works out its structures, there could be direct and constant collaboration between them and the mission-sending groups organized here. What is being done in the ecumenical area could well be a pattern for the interaction of episcopal commissions and various areas of the mission societies. Here, gathered with experts and experience, regular dialogue would be possible. Only in this way can be engendered the kind of creative thinking that is imperative. Only in this way can there be developed the full utilization of corporate resources that is so desperately required. The religious communities of the United States engaged in far-flung mission activity offer to the bishops a tremendous potential to fulfill their collegial responsibility. As in so many other things today, cooperation is of the essence. Resources, manpower, creative thinking are at a premium; the task is enormous, the problem explosive. Hence the spirit of collegiality, which is a spirit of common service in love, must seize upon us all.

The exercise of collegial responsibility in the mission areas themselves is already a fact—witnessed to by a growing number of efforts by individual dioceses. I think these are prophetic of the future and I need not enumerate them for you to whom they are well known.

[6] Louis and André Rétif, *The Church's Mission in the World,* Twentieth Century Encyclopedia of Catholicism, Vol. 102 (New York, Hawthorn, 1962), pp. 89-90.

Rather I have given almost exclusive stress to collegial responsibility on the local and national level, since it is here that the power to define the future lies, it seems to me. The re-evaluation of the missionary problem, re-education in the total meaning of mission for the whole people of God, development of structures of cooperation, these are imperative and primary. Only if there is a revivification of necessary commitment on every level of the Church's existence can mission action on the collegial level be transformed from a stream to a mighty tide.

CONCLUSION

In concluding this chapter on the collegial responsibility for the needy churches, I should like to hark back to a point I made earlier. It is the fact that, underlying this movement of men toward unity, there is a growing awareness of a body of common human values joined to a determination to incarnate them in their new societies. It is in this area that a singular opportunity and a singular challenge is open to collegial responsibility on both the national and local level. Yet, at the same time, it looks directly to the universal mission of the Church. For these human values that make possible freedom and dignity are a deep Christian concern and are frequently of Christian origin. As Pope John noted: "The Church, Her youth ever renewed by the breath of the Spirit, is always ready to recognize, to witness and even to quicken all that honors human intelligence and the human heart." But more than this is needed now, for Christians everywhere must revere and incarnate these values in so manifest a way that they become a flesh and blood proof of the truth of the Gospel. Thus it could well be that Selma is the significant missionary event of our time.

Above all, what is most needed is a spirituality of mission welling up from a vision of the world marching toward its common goal. Something of this is beautifully and prophetically described in the very ancient Shepherd of Hermas. The Shepherd sees a tower quarried from twelve mountains and he is told that these mountains represent the twelve nations of the world to whom the Apostles had preached. He asks how is it that while mountains are different shapes and colors, yet when built up into the tower they are all one color, and the Lord replies:

> The reason is that all the nations that dwell beneath the sky when once they heard the Gospel and believed were called in the name of the Son of God. In receiving the seal, they took on one mind and one spirit, in the unity of one faith and spirit of love. . . . In this way the tower came to be built of one color and shone like the sun (Sim. 9, c. 17, 1-4).

Individual and Group Responsibility for the Needy Churches

JOHN A. BELL, W.F.

It has become almost commonplace to assert in missionary gatherings that we stand on the threshold of a new era in the Church's perennial mission to the world. And yet, in any discussion of our individual and collective responsibility for this mission it is necessary to begin with this salient fact of contemporary history.

We are now witnessing deep sociological changes within the Church and the world in general. Some of these changes are already clearly visible; others we can sense without as yet being able to ascertain their exact nature or the exact direction in which they are propelling mankind, and consequently the Church. But we must prepare ourselves for the new dimensions of our responsibility by being attentive to all the indications of these changes.

In the past, we have been content with a one-dimensional pastoral theology: based upon tradition and past experience. We have now reached the stage of developing a two-dimensional pastoral theology: one which takes into account the reality of contemporary situations as well as the wisdom of experience. But to be really effective in the modern world, our pastoral approach must become three-dimensional: taking into account the directions of future change as well as present situations and past experience.

What are the indications that we have at our disposal for reflection upon an evaluation of our present and future responsibilities?

First of all we have the Council, which we have come to realize is much more than the deliberations of the bishops and other Council Fathers in Rome. The whole Church is, so to speak, in a state of Council at the present time, with repercussions affecting all Christians and even all mankind, although these periphery effects will take more time to become fully evident.

The work of the Council has already produced a decided shift in the Church's center of gravity. In an address last year to the Major Superiors of Belgium, Father Schillebeeckx described this shift (or "decentration," as he called it) as the Council's central theme. He enumerated five directions which this shift is taking:

1. A shift from *the Church* considered as an independent entity toward Christ, of whom the Church is a sign. "The center of interest of the faithful is shifted from the Church, from the Holy Father and the episcopate as a whole, toward Christ."[1] Pope Paul's pilgrimage to the Holy Land was a symbolic act of Rome rededicating herself to Christ.

2. A decentralization in Church government permitting a larger participation of the episcopate in the

[1] Edward Schillebeeckx, O.P., *Collaboration of Religious among Themselves, with the Episcopacy and with Secular Priests.* 1965, p. 4.

government of the Church. This is the most obvious of the five changes.

3. A *decentration* away from the hierarchical office to the people of God so that authority in the Church is seen as a service for the faithful. "The collegial government of the Church by all the bishops in union with the pope is but a service—vested with authority—for the people of God. The center of all ecclesial life is not the hierarchy, but the people of God."[2]

4. A *decentration* of the entire Roman Catholic Church toward the other Christian Churches, toward Israel, and toward the world's other major religions.

5. Not so much a displacement as a deeper concern for the world and its worldly problems.

Father Schillebeeckx elaborated further: "All the way down the line the Church is undergoing a decentration; she is made a servant; a servant of religious and temporal humanity. There was talk of 'triumphalism in the Church.' It was said (at the Council) that, especially in its hierarchical government, the Church had made Herself too much the center, as if all the people of God were at the service of the hierarchy, whereas the contrary is the truth. The Church acted as though She were a static value, changeless as a block of granite, while the evolution of the world and the ferment of the ages passed by. She Herself remained calmly erect without in any way being carried along in the whirlpool of time. The Church was too little the landmark it should have been, pointing toward Christ and toward the people of God."[3]

[2] *Ibid.*, p. 7.
[3] *Ibid.*, p. 8.

This, I think, aptly describes the attitudes which are generating the pastoral and sociological changes beginning to be felt in the Church and which will certainly continue at an ever-increasing tempo.

These considerations may seem rather far removed from this morning's topic. However, I think they form the essential background for any reflection on our own particular responsibilities for the needy churches.

To complete the picture, and at the risk of repeating things with which many of us are familiar, I would like to point briefly to some of the major changes that have occurred in our apostolate to the non-Christian world.

The last four centuries have seen the Church spread beyond the historical limits of Christendom to cover the entire world. This evangelization of non-European peoples was carried on by relatively small groups of missionaries, practically all members of religious orders. During the age of exploration and the beginnings of European colonialism, it was members of the already existing orders of men who accompanied the explorers, the military commanders, and the merchant convoys—Franciscans, Dominicans, Carmelites, and Augustinians—along with the newcomers in the field, the Jesuits. Their mission derived from the Holy See but also from the temporal powers, the Catholic kings of Spain and Portugal. St. Francis Xavier went to India with a double title: Apostolic Nuncio and Special Envoy of the King of Portugal. Propaganda Fide was founded in 1622, but it has only been in the last hundred years or so that Rome has in fact exercised effective control over the work of evangelization. The right of patronage, originally granted to the Catholic kings and perpetuated in one form or another, continued to interfere with apostolic freedom for centuries, while many religious orders invoked prior privilege to preserve their independence from the Congregation's supervision and direction.

This intermingling of the spiritual and temporal spheres set a pattern for missionary work which was to endure—with some attenuations, of course—practically to the end of World War II.

All of this and other factors resulted in missionaries (and consequently the rest of the Church) conceiving their mission as one of expanding the frontiers of Christendom, of assimilating non-Christian peoples to the civilization of Europe as well as to its religion. Missionary work took on the aspect of the new Crusades, in which valiant missionaries, heirs to the crusading spirit that had freed the Iberian peninsula from the Moors, embarked on the spiritual conquest of new lands and peoples. During the nineteenth century, several specialized congregations and societies devoted exclusively, or almost exclusively, to foreign mission work were founded to keep pace with the increasing tempo of evangelization in non-Christian areas, while the twentieth century has seen the establishment of at least eight national foreign mission societies.

Evangelization has been most successful among peoples of a comparatively low culture: in the Americas, Africa, and Oceania. For here, assimilation to European culture has been more or less accepted as a positive value by the people. Wherever missionaries encountered a highly integrated, self-sufficient culture, their most devoted efforts have met with little success.

Misgivings with regard to the general policy of assimilation were strongly expressed by such men as Valignano, Ricci, and De Nobili. But, despite their splendid example, the policy of assimilation triumphed, with the consequences that we are still experiencing today.

Radical changes, however, have taken place in the last few decades. First of all, the period of the geographic expansion of the Church has ended. There are, of course, a few small areas of the world where the Gospel has not yet been preached, either because they are remote and sparsely populated or because political restrictions have prevented a missionary presence.

CULTURAL PENETRATION

This implantation of the Church of Christ throughout the world does not mean that we have evangelized the world. Far from it. We have now come face-to-face with an immense problem of cultural penetration. After several centuries of evangelization, there are only 1.8 per cent Catholics in areas where Buddhism is the dominant religious culture; 1.32 per cent in Hindu areas; 1.03 per cent for Muslim areas, and only .3 per cent for Shinto areas.[4] Sub-Saharan Africa is now experiencing a cultural renaissance which is going to confront us with the same problem of cultural penetration despite a Catholic population of about 9 per cent in this area.

We can either continue to chip away rather ineffectually at these culturally closed religious blocs or we

[4] Figures are from *Informations Catholiques Internationales,* Vol. 199 (Sept. 1, 1963), p. 16.

can turn our energy to devising means of penetrating their cultures so that Christianity can once more become the leaven in the dough that Christianized the Roman Empire and the Germanic tribes.

The problem of cultural penetration is not limited to the highly integrated religious culture blocs we have mentioned; it is now a world-wide phenomenon facing the Church everywhere—in the de-Christianized sectors of Europe, in the ever-growing urban conglomerations of Latin America, and here in the United States among our Negro population as well as in affluent suburbia.

Another aspect of the new situation is a broader, more open concept of the Church's mission to the world. Today's missioner cannot ignore the themes of Pope John's *Mater et Magistra* and *Pacem in Terris* or Pope Paul's *Ecclesiam Suam,* nor those of the Constitution on the Church.

Finally, one more aspect of the new situation is the ever-increasing involvement of the entire Church in the work of evangelization. Preaching the Gospel to non-Christians is no longer exclusively the work of a small group of specialists. Today a religious community without any missionary commitment somewhere is regarded as a black sheep. More and more diocesan priests are being lent to the young churches by their bishops. There are about 200 U.S. diocesan priests serving in Latin America. There are well over 200 European diocesan priests working in mission dioceses of Africa, although I know of only three American diocesan priests in Africa (and two of them are working for Catholic Relief Services). The number of lay missionaries, both members of associations and "free lancers," has steadily increased since World War II.

EPISCOPAL INVOLVEMENT

The most recent phenomenon in this sphere is episcopal involvement in the Church's missionary effort.

In the developing churches, the growth of a normal hierarchy, that is to say, one chosen from among diocesan priests of that country and culture, means a shift in responsibility from a missionary group to a diocesan bishop. Even where the bishop is still an expatriate missionary or a native member of a religious community, he now thinks and reacts more as a residential bishop than as a missionary or religious. The growth of national episcopal conferences has brought local bishops and bishops of different religious societies into closer relations with each other so that they have become aware of their existence as a national hierarchy. All this is a normal development in the life of these maturing churches.

The Council has accelerated the pace of contacts between the bishops of the needy churches and those of the affluent churches. Contacts between episcopal conferences and the twinning of dioceses are reenforcing the trend.

Mission bishops are less dependent upon provincials of the order which has evangelized their territory. Formerly, the bishop looked almost exclusively to the provincial, to the mission procurator, and the vocation director for his supply of funds and personnel. When Sisters or Brothers were needed to staff an institution in a diocese, the contact was most often made either by the provincial or at least with his help.

Now bishops in the mission-sending countries are becoming more responsive to appeals made directly to them by their fellow bishops, whom they are beginning to know personally. More and more individual dioceses are being placed on missionary cooperation plans, where formerly it was only the religious communities which appealed for their missions.

A step forward in episcopal cooperation in this country was achieved when the American bishops answered the Holy See's appeal and organized themselves to extend fraternal assistance to their brother bishops of Latin America. However, it cannot compare with what European hierarchies have done and are already planning for the future. The achievements of the German church through the Misereor and Adveniat campaigns are a great example of what a hierarchy can achieve when it becomes fully mission-minded.

All of these are signs of a slow but sure shift in responsibility for evangelization away from the traditional missionary societies to the hierarchy, which is becoming conscious of its collegial nature as never before since the early days of the Church.

MISSION SOCIETIES NEEDED?

The question, therefore, arises: What will be the future role of the mission-sending society in the new era of evangelization we are now entering? One thing is certain: it will not be the same as in the past; and the problem before us is to begin delineating the pattern of future responsibility. This pattern partially depends upon the role of religious communities in the Church of the future, and unfortunately, this is anything but clear at the present time.

In Europe, a significant number of people are asking if there is still a need for missionary societies in the Church. As the bishops and their priests and people start to assume their responsibilities for the apostolate throughout the world, missionary societies will become superfluous, some say. This line of reasoning is so widespread that one of the major addresses at the Louvain Missiology Week in 1965 was entitled: "Are Missionary Institutes Still Needed in the Church?"

This question is especially important for those societies and congregations of men or of women which are exclusively missionary in scope and activity. It is not merely their future role in mission work that is being questioned, but their very existence. If they are no longer needed in the traditional mission areas, if the bishops of the world and diocesan priests can carry on the assistance which the needy churches require and expect, then the missionary societies must either orient themselves to other pastoral activities in the Church (which would, in reality, be going against the original charism of their founders) or cease to exist.

The question is not, therefore, a purely academic one, but one which must be faced squarely. For the answers given will help to indicate more concretely our own particular responsibilities in the future.*

* [Ed. Note: The Decree on the Missionary Activity of the Church, since published, answered this question: ". . . these institutes remain extremely necessary." See especially No. 27.]

The problem has two aspects: the new role of the mission-sending society within the needy churches and, secondly, its role in a developed church which, conscious of its world-wide responsibilities, is entering what is now called "a state of mission."

In order to understand the role of mission-sending societies in the needy churches, one must keep in mind several distinctions.

First of all, there is a difference in approach between exclusively missionary societies and other religious orders and congregations exercising a missionary function.

Exclusively missionary societies cannot rightly seek to perpetuate themselves in the newly established churches in the same way as other religious societies. They cannot be true to their particular charismatic function in the Church if they attempt to establish themselves in mission lands by large-scale recruiting, the opening of training houses, etc., in view of the permanent erection of a province of their society in Central Africa, or in Japan, or in Bolivia. This does not mean that individuals from mission areas who seem to have been given an authentic missionary vocation cannot be accepted as members of that society, but they must really be missionaries in spirit and ready to leave their own country and culture according to the needs of the universal Church.

On the other hand, religious communities whose charismatic function in the Church is broader than missionary activity in a strict sense can legitimately seek to recruit candidates in a mission land in view of erecting a permanent province of their order. For even if they have been extensively engaged in missionary activity and have in fact been the agents of the Church's missionary expansion in that area, one can foresee a permanent function to be exercised by a local province even after the church there has reached a stage of mature development. This would be the case of congregations of teaching Brothers and Sisters, for example, or for Franciscans, Dominicans, Jesuits, and all the other societies whose work in the Church is in reality broader than the evangelization of non-Christian peoples.

However, even in such cases, it is necessary for their major superiors to explore carefully, in collaboration with the local hierarchy, how their particular charism can be exercised to the maximum in the service of that cultural penetration I have previously mentioned. It is not sufficient to merely transplant personnel from America or Europe to the needy churches so that they can continue to work along traditional lines. Nor is it justified to perpetuate oneself in a new church uniquely for one's own sake when the foundation of an independent local congregation would seem to be more indicated by concrete conditions.

Let me give you an example of the study and reflection that are needed in this area. The Capuchins in the Congo have just ordained their first four Congolese priests. They are now asking themselves whether or not they should seek to introduce into central Africa the style of life led by St. Francis and the early Franciscans. Traveling bands of preachers living in villages among the people rather than in monasteries, ministering to the sick, to those in prison, living on alms from the local people or by manual work. Not engaging in strictly parochial work, but revaluating the original Franciscan charism in the present-day conditions of central Africa which, from a sociological and religious point of view, resemble more the Europe of the Middle Ages in which the Franciscan ideal was born than our present Western world.[5]

NEW IDEAS

In this respect there is a need for bold and imaginative thinking. It must be based on shrewd observation of conditions and future trends in these developing nations as well as upon real research in depth into the methods used during the centuries of Christian cultural penetration of Europe. Much from the missionary past of the Church can be resurrected and adapted to our current situations or, at least, will be suggestive of new approaches. All too often we limit our view of past experience, or of what is traditional, to the last few centuries only, overlooking the riches contained in the more distant patrimony of the Church.

A second distinction necessary for evaluating our responsibilities is that of the various ministries to be exercised within the needy churches.

There is, first of all, the need to supplement the present insufficiency of clergy and religious in these churches so as to provide for the pastoral care of the growing Catholic population. In almost every area, vocations have not kept pace with conversions. Second-

[5] See *Documentation and Information for and about Africa.* Leopoldville, 1965, No. 149-150.

and third-generation Catholics must receive an integral Christian formation and education. And here, in parentheses, we should ask ourselves whether a Catholic school system as it has been developed in the Church during the past few centuries is the real answer to this need.[6]

Secondly, we have the whole field of ecumenical contacts and relations which up to now have hardly been considered a distinct ministry within the Church. In the future, this work will have to be carefully distinguished from the apostolate to non-Christians. There are many initiatives that can be taken in this field because ecumenism has quite a different aspect once one leaves the geographic and cultural areas in which the struggles of the Reformation and the Counter-Reformation took place.

Thirdly, there is the field of social action which in line with recent papal social teaching must henceforth be considered as a ministry or service of the people of God to humanity.[7] Here again new, creative thinking is needed in the developing nations. Our social action must be carefully preserved from all forms of sectarianism. It must be elaborated in broad and fruitful collaboration with other Christian bodies, with non-Christian groups, and with national and international agencies.

I have kept for last what is the essential ministry of missionary activity, the evangelization of non-Chris-

[6] On this question see D. W. Robinson, M.M., "The Church, Schools and Religious Liberty," *African Ecclesiastical Review*, Vol. 7 (Jan. 1965), pp. 9-22.

[7] See Joseph Gremillion, *The Other Dialogue* (Garden City, Doubleday, 1965).

tians and the necessary condition for its success in the future: cultural penetration by the Church of the great non-Christian cultures of the world. There are ever-growing areas in Africa where evangelization has been drastically curtailed as a result of the pressures of the pastoral ministry to Catholics. Similarly, in Latin America the revitalization of Catholic life and practice and the rapid increase in population have brought about the same difficulties, which will become more and more acute until the rate of new vocations can begin to catch up with the needs of the pastoral ministry.

We have hardly begun to tackle the immense task of developing both the rationale and the concrete means of that cultural penetration which is essential to the mission of the Church in our modern world. Everything that is profoundly human and good in a given milieu must be fully assimilated; its mentality, its sensibilities, its language. The positive preparation for the Gospel (*preparatio evangelica*) found in a greater or lesser degree in every culture must be discovered and made use of in a judicious manner. The human anxieties and longings concealed in apparent cultural complacency must be brought to light so that the message of Christ may be seen as the only complete answer to deep human aspirations.

This massive effort to understand, to adapt, to compenetrate is the key to effective evangelization. All of us will readily admit this on the speculative plane, but we must ask ourselves if we are really committed to it in action. Are we striving to distinguish the essence of God's revelation to men from the Western cultural forms in which it has been preached and lived by men of Western culture? We have been presenting the divine message in an envelope which is Western European (and often not of recent vintage). The majority of non-Western peoples are either repulsed by the envelope or just not interested in it. Our task is to break open the envelope so that the message can be seen for what it really is—the loving solicitude of God, Creator and Redeemer, for all men of all cultures to unite them all in Christ, who calls no particular culture His own.

The cultural penetration I am speaking of requires that individual missionaries be trained to enter effectively into new cultures and to operate efficiently within them; but it means much more than that. It means moving the entire institutional Church structure in a non-Western country from a Western cultural content into the indigenous culture. This move must, of course, not be violent; it has to follow the rhythm of growth and change; it has to be coordinated by the hierarchy but without suppressing legitimate and controlled initiative and experimentation.

It requires a lot of preliminary research which has yet to be done. There are the beginnings of a few efforts in various parts of Africa, in India, and in southeast Asia, but the furthest advanced in this area is the Oriens Institute for Religious Research in Tokyo under the direction of Father Joseph Spae, C.I.C.M., whom many of you know.[8]

This long, patient work of cultural penetration, as well as the evangelization of non-Christians which we

[8] See Joseph Spae, C.I.C.M., *Christian Corridors to Japan* (Tokyo, Oriens Institute for Religious Research, 1965).

can now see as a highly specialized work, amply justifies the continued existence in the Church of specialized missionary societies which can provide Her with men and women who have committed themselves for life to these tasks. It is within such a framework (and that also provided by other orders with major missionary commitments) that the expertise needed for this work can best be developed and channeled.

This enumeration of the various ministries needed in the developing churches is not intended to be exhaustive. It is sufficient, however, to show that there are several easily distinguishable areas of activity, all of which are necessary for a well-balanced apostolic strategy. No one individual can be equally competent in all these areas and, consequently, choices have to be made not only by individuals but also by communities. Talents, resources, and charisms have to be assessed. The priorities within a particular church have to be studied in conjunction with the bishop and his advisors so that a sound plan in view of the common good can be elaborated.

In conclusion, let us now turn our attention briefly to the role of the mission-sending societies in the developed churches. Until very recent times, these societies have been the main source of support for the Church's work of evangelization. During the modern period of missionary expansion, the role of the hierarchy in this work has been mainly permissive. Bishops have been exhorted by the Holy See to establish and encourage the work of the Pontifical Mission Aid Societies on both a national and a diocesan level and to permit in their dioceses missionary recruitment and fund-raising by the mission-sending societies. However, with rare exceptions, they have not taken an active part in seeking funds and personnel for the Church's mission activity.

COOPERATION

The Constitution *De Ecclesia* tells us "that the individual bishops, insofar as their own discharge of their duty permits, are obliged to enter into a community of work among themselves and with the successor of Peter, upon whom was imposed in a special way the great duty of spreading the Christian name. With all their energy, therefore, they must supply to the missions both workers for the harvest and also spiritual and material aid, both directly and on their own account, as well as by arousing the ardent cooperation of the faithful" (*De Ecclesia,* No. 23).

This means that new forms of cooperation must be found. And as in any new relationship being elaborated, there are dangers that must be avoided. It would be truly lamentable if some bishops were to feel that their collegial responsibility meant that the Church's missionary effort should henceforth be their sole responsibility, that it should be "diocesanized," so to speak. Such an attitude would in fact deny to the people of God their rights to exercise the apostolate and would tend to stifle the charismatic life of the Church which for centuries has found expression in religious orders and congregations, most of whom have received their founding inspiration from simple priests or from the faithful, rather than from the hierarchy.[9]

Perhaps more dangerous is the possibility that the mission-sending societies may approach the problem on the defensive, with distrust, quick to resent any interference in a domain that has been traditionally theirs. The history of the early days of the Congregation of Propaganda Fide shows that this is not an illusory danger.

What is needed is an open, loyal, and sincere dialogue between the bishops and the major superiors of mission-sending societies to explore the ways and means of collaborating together to transform the church in the United States into a church "in the state of mission." I would even go so far as to suggest that our major superiors take the initiative in opening this dialogue. As superiors of religious communities, they represent "a vital expression of the charismatic and prophetic character of the Church." For each religious community approved by the hierarchy is, in fact, an institutionalized charism whose ecclesial character has been recognized as a positive contribution to the life of the Church.[10] A certain healthy tension, an interaction between the hierarchical function of authority and the charismatic function, is necessary for the work of renewal in the Church.

All of us here today, either because of our past service in the mission fields or because of our commitment of one sort or another to the Church's missionary

[9] Schillebeeckx, *op. cit.*, pp. 11-19.
[10] *Ibid.*, pp. 11-12.

work, are especially fitted to promote a sense of mission within the various dioceses of our country.

We have the prophetic mission within the American church to bear witness to its Catholicity, to the universality of God's call to salvation, to the obligation of the people of God to evangelize the world. It is not the bishops alone who are burdened with this responsibility; it is ours as well.

So often have I heard people complain that if we wait for the bishops to act, we will wait a long time. Let us not waste our time in sterile laments that advance nothing. Let us rather, through the proper channels, put ourselves wholeheartedly at the service of the hierarchy and ask them to use our talents and experience in replying to this challenging opportunity.

Perhaps the greatest service that we as missionaries can render to the needy churches at the present time is to be the catalysts within American Catholicism which will enable our bishops to communicate to their people the dynamic, fruitful vision of the Church contained in *De Ecclesia:* ". . . that messianic people, although it does not actually include all men, and at times may look like a small flock, is nonetheless a lasting and sure seed of unity, hope, and salvation for the whole human race. Established by Christ as a communion of life, charity, and truth, it is also used by Him as an instrument for the redemption of all, and is sent forth into the whole world as the light of the world and the salt of the earth" (*De Ecclesia,* No. 9).

COOPERATION: The Key to Apostolic Action

J. Gerard Grondin, M. M.

In view of the dynamism in the Church it is inconceivable that we have not spent a great deal of time thinking and talking about cooperation. Then why is it necessary to discuss it again? Simply because we are growing, we are developing, and we need to assimilate gradually the wonderful ideas and ideals which God is showing us so brightly that we are in danger of being blinded and a little frightened. The renewal of Pentecost is always awesome and good for one's humility.

We missionaries have been humiliated in various degrees all over the world. While we are proud of our martyrs, proud of our calling, ever more fervently dedicated to our work, we know that the world has turned brilliant and critical lights upon our weaknesses and judged us sometimes harshly, usually with some foundation. More often we have been judged with admirable kindness and consideration because of our good intentions.

These attacks of others in all their variegated shades of censure, pity, contempt, envy perhaps, can be useful, provided we ourselves weigh the conclusions of our critics against the criteria which we hold true. Constructive criticism and cooperative planning will help us find cures for our weaknesses and lead us to more truly Christian ways of life.

We have a lot to learn from one another. Our ideas become clarified through acting with one another. For example, you may have to meditate before achieving understanding of what is meant when the bishops of one country unanimously assert that to use social activities, such as education, medical facilities, social services, in an opportunist way, as a shortcut to conversions, is an indefensible diversion of the immediate aims of these essentially temporal activities, and could endanger very seriously the essential freedom and necessarily supernatural motives of the act of faith.

We have a richness of new circumstances in the world, new ideas emanating from all sides. Not so many years ago we probably would have devised neat categories to classify people of varying beliefs as friends or foes and gone peacefully on our own way. This is no longer possible. The relationships between nations and religions and persons are becoming so complex that we can no longer live apart. We Christians are forced to become a true leaven, a salt of the earth.

To take advantage of this great missionary opportunity we must be aware that we too have changed, that even the words we use have acquired new meanings.

Take the phrase, "mission-sending society." At one time this term may have seemed to apply only to small specialized groups within the Church. The Second Vatican Council has speeded the day when every Christian society will be in some way a sending society and inevitably a receiving society, therefore a cooperating society.

Many of us have begun to use the words "new breed" in missionary circles and we like to think of these words as relating to renewal and refreshing updating. When so used, the words "new breed" have no connotation of brash youth or bitter old revolutionaries as opposed to despairing weaklings, old or young. This is a breed found in all walks of life, people who are beginning to feel happy and confident in a dynamic world of apparently limitless possibilities for development, a breed stable enough to rejoice in constant change, in vital mutation.

Take the word "ferment." All over the world there is ferment, a working of ideas and a disturbance of human living which produce some fogginess and confusion but, you know, the marvelous phenomenon of it all is that the sprouts of consensus are beginning to be seen. Soon these sprouts of consensus will be trees, as the parable tells us. Structures of consensus are being built first of all in the Second Vatican Council and in many other important meetings, for example the Christopher Study Week on "Apostolic Renewal in the Seminary." This consensus, if carefully nurtured, can cross the boundaries of nationality, overcome the isolating powers of the elements, and prepare the new home of the family of God, nibbling away at provincialism, regional denominationalism, egocentrism.

Yes, we need to discuss again cooperation, to consider the fundamental principles on which our plans for cooperation should be based, namely the nature of the Church and the nature of man. We also need to analyze some of the essential qualities of such cooperation, such as freedom and courage.

BASIS FOR COOPERATION

Nature of the Church: In the Constitution *De Ecclesia* one idea seems to have elicited much study and discussion and that is collegiality. Collegiality is for us a relatively new concept; it will be some time before all the implications for the missions will be clarified. It is already clear that the bishops, with the Holy Father, are the highest authority in all things pertaining to the mission of the Church. However, every member of the Church shares this duty. Each individual person must show some personal initiative and responsibility, make his personal and particular contribution in accord with the less particular directives which come from the bishops. From the theological point of view, the full meaning of collegiality is not restricted to cooperation among the bishops. There are theological indications that the reality of collegiality extends to all the institutions and even individual members of the Church. It would even be true in some sense to say that the collegiality of the bishops rests on the reality of the common interests of the particular churches.

It is also clear that our mission-sending groups are at the service of societies higher than our own societies in the hierarchical structure of the Church. Obviously we are at the service of our own conference of bishops. Many of us are likely to be placed directly at the service of the hierarchy of some other country and, of course, all are subject to the supreme authority of the

Church, the college of bishops under the direction of the Holy Father. This hierarchical structure is a reminder that the ideal cooperative action is not merely a result of modern complex circumstances, but a consequence of the nature of the Church established by Christ, who is the Head of the Church. As the Constitution says: From Him

> "the whole body, supplied and built up by joints and ligaments, attains a growth that is of God" (Col. 2:19). He continually distributes in His body, that is, in the Church, gifts of ministries in which, by His own power, we serve each other unto salvation so that, carrying out the truth in love, we might through all things grow unto Him who is our Head. . . . This Church constituted and organized in the world as a society, subsists in the Catholic Church, which is governed by the successor of Peter and by the bishops in communion with him, although many elements of sanctification and of truth are found outside of its visible structure. These elements, as gifts belonging to the Church of Christ, are forces impelling toward Catholic unity (*De Ecclesia,* Nos. 7, 8).

Thus it is that we who wish to serve Christ more devotedly and effectively in the missionary field must be aware of the social nature of the Church, and of its essential direction toward unity—a unity which is strengthened and beautified by coordinated diverse activities, which are nothing else than what we call cooperation.

We should also be very mindful of the need for cooperation which arises from the rights of the Church abroad. We are but part of the people of God. There are many nationalities in the people of God. We will encounter these different nationalities in the people of God. We will encounter these different nationalities in our work. Not only the hierarchy of these other nations will have a right to direct us, but the priests and religious and laity of these other nationalities will have the right and indeed the duty to scrutinize our mission methods, to praise and to criticize our programs, to intervene and caution when our human weakness or even selfishness is retarding the growth of the Church and marring its perfection. We may resent this wholesome cooperation, we may deem it interference. At times our fellow apostles abroad may be unreasonable, but certainly we must accept unequivocally the need for us to try to work harmoniously with them.

Another point made by the Constitution refers to our obligation, in a spirit of solidarity with all human beings, to work at making the world a more just and reasonable environment for the Kingdom of God. We will have to cooperate with those citizens who are not yet visibly members of the people of God. The Church is messianic. The Church cannot go its own way without reference to the attitudes and legitimate aspirations of the whole of the human race. We Christians are in the world and it is our duty, especially of the laity, to help create a better world. The Constitution says:

> Therefore, by their competence in secular training and by their activity, elevated from within by the grace of Christ, let them vigorously contribute their

> effort, so that created goods may be perfected by human labor, technical skill, and civic culture for the benefit of all men according to the design of the Creator and the light of His Word. May the goods of this world be more equitably distributed among all men, and may they in their own way be conducive to universal progress in human and Christian freedom (*De Ecclesia,* No. 36).

The Constitution has much more to say about this duty to better the world. Reread it at your leisure but remember this: the days of basket weaving are over and the Christians of the world as citizens must work and cooperate with all who genuinely wish to improve the world.

This earthly wisdom is acquired only by hard work and a respect for science and technical excellence. The missionary, ordained, religious, or lay, is not necessarily or even usually the technician best suited to solve the problems of the temporal world, but the missionary must work at it, respect the dignity of temporal endeavors, and do his share according to circumstances. This too is a normal part of one's missionary life.

We must make the words of the Preface for the Mass of Christ the King come true: "An everlasting kingdom of truth and life, a kingdom of holiness and grace, a kingdom of justice, love, and peace."

Nature of Man: Since not all men are visible members of the Church, and not all men agree with what Catholics hold to be true concerning the nature of the Church, we need a common ground with others on which to base our attempts at cooperation for common goals. This we find in our common human nature.

As our knowledge and understanding of one another grows throughout the world we find ever-increasing hope for solutions to our differences. Human beings in all their splendid variety are members of the one human race and we must progress toward the basic unity which is the consequence of our creation and development through the Word of God.

Our fellow Christians who are not Catholic have a wonderful sense of the Church as community, and while at times we think of them as excessively individualistic, they are in fact very conscious of the need for dialogue and cooperation.

Cooperation with the citizens of developing countries has many possibilities and problems, but it cannot be denied that in some circumstances cooperation is not only the best but actually the only avenue open to apostolic action for two very understandable reasons. First of all, the citizens of these developing countries have been at times scandalized and disillusioned by all our Christian divisions. We must not willfully perpetuate this scandal.

Second, the sincere leaders of the less privileged countries have an intense sense of urgency about the material needs of their people, such as sickness, illiteracy, poverty. Many of these leaders believe in democracy and personal freedom as deeply as you and I, but they consider their countries to be in a state of emergency, comparable to war, when sacrifies must be made for the common good even at the cost of some personal privileges and less urgent needs. This attitude of the leaders can give an appearance of Fascism or Communism to developing countries, an appearance which it is very important to distinguish from real Fascism or Communism as ideologies.

The fact is that most countries urgently need advance in socialization. This may take the form of communalism in Africa, or Christianized socialism in Latin America, but the fact remains that cooperation and understanding is indispensable to a relevant apostolate in these areas.

Cooperation in states associating with Communism presents us with various degrees of difficulty, and perplexing problems in deciding how far one can go before one risks compromising the faith or falling into the hands of real enemies. However, it seems clear to me that there are grave mistakes made by people of good will who label as Communistic every social action which goes against the status quo and disturbs the apparent peace of structures that are to some extent unjust. Ghana and Indonesia are countries where the Catholic Church is conducting a very edifying apostolate even though there are people in this country who fear them as committed to atheistic Communism. Bolivia has had disturbances which have been labeled Communistic, when in fact the cassock was about the only passport and guarantee of safe conduct recognized by rioters. This has also been true in Tanzania. It can become a bit ridiculous when people close their eyes to all the shades of ideology and separate themselves categorically from the possibilities of apostolic action among those who need it most. Such conduct may be good political action; it is not apostolic action.

It is important that we continue to improve the possibilities for cooperation in our world. Some cooperation is necessary for man's perfection. This is the inevitable consequence of man's social nature given to us that we might reflect the complex life of the Trinity. Man perfects himself by acting socially. To be useful, to feel friendship and love, to share in noble accomplishments are needs of our human nature. Ideas, culture, faith can be shared without depriving oneself of any treasure. Quite the contrary; sound social activity enriches the person, and is mentioned often in the Scriptures as a source of grace and glory for mankind. All this is necessary preparation for the development of the Kingdom of God.

ESSENTIAL QUALITIES OF COOPERATION

It would be shortsighted to stress the unifying aspects of the nature of the Church and of the nature of man as ordained by God without bringing them into focus with the essential qualities of human nature which bring tension between human beings who are working together. Cooperation must respect personal freedom and personal responsibility. Cooperation must allow for the exercise of initiative and courage. Cooperation is not synonymous with centralization or depersonalization.

Freedom: Christianity has placed great stress on the value of the individual and the sacredness of some of his rights. Much has been written about the principle of subsidiarity, which emphasizes the need of individuals and primary societies, such as the family, to fulfill their basic obligations without interference from broader societies and organizations, except in those cases where the individual or primary society is clearly unable to fulfill adequately their God-given functions. This same principle of subsidiarity must be applied to cooperation among the various groups from our country who seek to exercise a wholesome apostolic action overseas. Among us there are groups with special vocations and talents much as there are differences in our individual vocations and talents. It would be fatal if we envisaged cooperation as demanding that every society or group perform the same functions in the same way.

Religious orders and ecclesiastical societies have individualities which attract certain personalities. Secular groups differ in membership, aims, and methods. Lay people have a number of paths open to them for the apostolate. Dioceses which have become "sending-societies" have many alternatives to choose from. Any plan for cooperation must respect the legitimate aspirations of all these, and in fact foment them. Persons or societies do no wrong when they develop talents and skills or even resources greater than those of others. They do wrong only when they isolate themselves excessively and use God-given gifts in a selfish way for their private interests without thought or respect for the needs and rights of others on this increasingly complex planet. There is greater need for cooperation today precisely because the individuals in the world, and the societies in the world, are richer in knowledge and resources than ever before and their actions reverberate in ever-growing waves of influence.

People who pool their individual resources to achieve a common goal usually benefit individually, but at the same time they become dependent on their associates and they make themselves responsible for their associates in some way or other, thereby creating a whole new status implying rights and duties. The multiplication of these relationships should not be pushed to extremes. While it is true that cooperation is the clearly indicated will of God, it is also true that God leaves areas for the freedom of man to operate in, and we must view cooperation in this way—a free association of people helping one another to make our apostolic action more effective.

Pope John emphasized the reality of increasing socialization in the modern world. He presented to all of humanity the ideal of a way of life, a Christian morality which relates to widening circles of involvement and commitment. But he also defended "the freedom of individual citizens and groups of citizens to act autonomously, while cooperating one with another." It is now up to us to find concrete applications of these high ideals to our own particular position in life. Cooperation need not always be ordered or even directed from above by superiors, nor much less by committee chairmen. Superiors and committees will have a fruitful function in cooperation very much proportionate to the spirit of cooperation among the individuals in the groups which such superiors and committees serve.

Successful cooperation among mission-sending societies will depend on how successful we, subjects and leaders alike, are in visualizing and putting into practice the art of cooperation.

Therefore, cooperation is the key to apostolic action mostly because it is the key to all human achievement in our modern world. We in America have some of the attributes that make cooperation pleasant. We are friendly and helpful.

There is in all our mission-sending societies this individual basic good will to help which is the basis for all more complex types of cooperation. We want to be useful—we like to meet fellow-workers who share our problems. Our societies must allow personal initiative and sufficient experimentation in developing this spirit of cooperation beyond the stage of Christian greetings and hospitality. The trend of world events demands it. The trend in the Second Vatican Council demands it. I am convinced that world movements and the drives of Christian commitment are sufficiently strong to create a whole new concept of cooperation if our superiors are just a little permissive and generous in allowing and supporting this wider, more human, more Christlike way of life.

Many young people of today are attracted by the vision of teamwork more than by the image of rugged individualism. Young people do want to work together. As long as undue pressure is not imposed on them to conform to ideas or programs which they do not understand, they are quite prepared to make sacrifices to achieve a common goal. Among the older generation the young in spirit welcome a common effort to meet problems which they have had ample opportunity to observe and which they know will yield only to a concerted cooperative effort.

It seems to me that the tenor of these observations,

and they could be multiplied, shows that cooperation need not at all be a restriction of personal liberty. On the contrary, we are all beginning to accept freely the idea that cooperation is indeed the shortest route to achieve what we all desire, the extension and perfection of the Kingdom of God.

Courage: We missionaries know that every person who goes to a foreign country experiences a certain culture shock, a disheartening experience which results from a disruption of our habits—a more or less severe jarring of our way of thinking, an interruption of our manner of relaxing and enjoying life, a deviation from our way of working and getting things done, and inevitably a disturbance of our physical digestive systems. Similar phenomena await us as we seek to adapt our individualistic approach to life to a more socialized type of life. Fortunately, culture shock is a temporary thing. An easily understood proof that culture shock is temporary is the surprisingly intense desire of nearly all missionaries to remain in their countries of adoption. We do look forward to vacations and furloughs—we come home to visit our families and to seek help from all whom we can contact, but generally the main and dominating thought is an interest and concern for the people we leave behind in our missions.

Getting accustomed to cooperation launches us into the unknown, arouses some anxiety, and generally unnerves us in the early stages. Let me give you an example. About seven years ago the growing demands for education on the part of the people of Tanganyika, now called Tanzania since the merger with Zanzibar, made it imperative for individual dioceses and missionary groups to face up to the need for cooperative effort. We do not have the time to go into the many reasons for this conclusion, but it is a fact that all missioners concerned, Protestant as well as Catholic, recognized the compelling need to get together with the government and work out a cooperative solution. It was obvious to all that the common good of the people of Tanzania demanded this. We saw the need but we were anxious and not at all sure how to start. On the Catholic side some 18 dioceses, well over a dozen missionary orders or societies, a dozen nationalities, thousands of schools were involved. The same applied with unimportant differences to the Protestant groups.

As a start we organized special meetings of Catholic personnel to plan an approach. The Protestants did the same. We both had special committees to plan agendas acceptable to all parties—special committees to eliminate possible fiascos. We soon found out we had exaggerated the problems. Within two years we met formally and informally at all levels as though East Africa had never had a history of religious competition. We had made the transition and it is now difficult to understand the circumstances and causalities that made our previous attitudes possible. The cultural shock of interdenominational cooperation at the level of social services was short and cooperation has produced remarkably good results.

If we are to intensify our attitude of cooperation in our own country, we must have the courage to launch out bravely, with faith. This does not mean blindly, nor in a foolhardy manner. We know that differences of opinion exist within our own societies; we know that often there are a number of valid alternatives to choose from. We must be prepared to respect diversity and not fall into the trap of thinking that all must act in the same way. Excessive conformity is a mirage, not a goal to be sought for.

Also quite apart from legitimate differences we know that it is very human for factions to develop in all human enterprises. We must study the interplay of in-groups and out-groups, the tensions between liberty and authority, the dynamics of cultural change. We must be aware that the principles of community development in its broadest sense apply to our own modern institutions as well as to the primitive societies in which this science is usually studied. We must recognize that the science of management, on which our private enterprise is spending so much time and using great personnel, applies to all of us here present and is changing as rapidly as all other sciences in our modern world. We must have the courage to face up to these vital developments which affect our hopes and dreams of cooperation.

We must avoid the mistake of thinking that these principles are worldly principles, unworthy of our interest and dedicated attention. Good will and zeal are not enough for a relevant apostolate in the modern world.

Therefore, we need to be big enough to learn from others; we need to be alert and humble enough to recognize our mistakes; and we must be brave enough to risk making mistakes. Our world is changing—how often have we heard this truism. We will seldom have absolute certainty that we are doing the very best thing; the solutions of next year may not be adequate for the needs of the year after, but our progress has to be made year by year and our programs tested in the fire of experience.

Who bears the responsibility for bringing this spirit of cooperation into the apostolate? Who is to turn the key to success in apostolic action? Bishops and superiors have this obligation. The encouragement of conferences and unions of religious, so obvious in the present policies of the Church, makes this clear. But all of us share this obligation. Just as every human being has a freedom of choice, so each of us has a personal responsibility to foster the apostolic principle of cooperation. It is a sublime, never-ending challenge, for the exercise of social relationships is a part of the perfection of man—and there will always be room for improvement. It is a challenge which affects all ranks, in most of their activities. It is my job and yours.

SPECIAL AREAS OF COOPERATION

The mission-sending societies have been meeting for a number of years and have been discussing with one another a number of very pressing problems common to us all. The discussions have begun to bear fruit and I am confident that more and more concrete examples of actual cooperation will come into existence. There are three very special questions which I would like to touch upon briefly.

RESEARCH

> CARA is the Center for Applied Research in the Apostolate and its goal is to discover, promote, and apply modern techniques and scientific informational resources for practical use in a coordinated and effective approach to the Church's social and religious mission in the modern world . . . Countless years and lives are being wasted, and thousands of dollars are being foolishly disposed of in the Church's efforts because not enough research enters into apostolic activities.

The above sentences are quoted from a progress report made in May 1965 by Rev. Louis J. Luzbetak, the Administrator of CARA. I want to say that CARA can become one of the most significant institutions in our country from the point of view of the missions. In order to be good missionaries it is extremely important that we begin by understanding the nature of our own apostolate in this country. We must learn to distinguish what is essentially apostolic in our activity and what is historical, cultural accretion—and we will not achieve this without study.

This by no means implies that CARA will not study the problems we may encounter overseas. The field of mission activity is the world and a world closing in on itself, but I do want to emphasize our need to know why we do things the way we do them in this country. We need to subject our church to intense examination and constructive criticism. Otherwise we may foolishly try to export to other countries programs which do not apply to other countries, or even, which would be a real calamity, try to transplant some of our mistakes overseas.

The Conferences of Major Superiors have shown courage and vision in helping to bring this tremendous project to life and it is up to every one of us to help keep it alive and disseminate the ideas and attitudes that will make this great institution a success. It is a costly enterprise, but one of the wisest investments ever made for the success of apostolic action. Indeed CARA needs more than money: it needs our enlightened cooperation. We must help supply the information needed. Much of the information needed is already in our files, or stowed away in the recesses of our corporate experiences and knowledge. Busy as all of you are, please share with CARA the riches of your knowledge. Do not begrudge CARA the time spent in interviews or in filling in questionnaires. Be generous. CARA deserves it.

The Place of Social Action in Apostolic Action: This question is a very actual problem in many countries. In a Christmas 1960 statement by the bishops of Tanzania they said: "Politics, political instruments or political power are not means of religious proselytism, nor are social action: education, medical facilities, social services, etc."

This sentence taken with the thoughts already mentioned in the introduction of this talk should be carefully meditated by all of us. I think I can safely say that we reject political pressure as an instrument of conversion. I am sure that not all missioners have learned to reject the pressure of social services as an instrument of conversion as unequivocally as have the bishops of Tanzania.

"Social action," says the bishops' statement, "has its own aim, the betterment of the human temporal order. Social action prepares the human temporal milieu for the reception of the message of Christ."

But, the bishops caution us, we must not try to short-cut the process of conversion "by seeking directly to win souls by the lure of any advantages in those fields"—for such motives could not be the foundation for the highest ideals of our faith.

None of this implies a rejection of social action. "Social action is an indirect apostolate, that is, an opportunity of indirectly preparing men's minds and hearts for the reception of the message of Christ, and even for their eventually entering the Church."

If we ponder these statements in connection with what I have reported to you earlier about the attitudes of sincere leaders in developing countries toward matters social, we will understand the timeliness of re-examining the function of many of our institutions and evaluating carefully their relation to apostolic action.

SPECIALIZATION

One of the effects of the tremendous increase of knowledge in all branches of study in our day is the need for continuing education for all in ever-narrowing fields, or in other words—specialization.

In some ways the days when the missionary had to be a jack-of-all-trades are going, and people tend to pay little attention to the person who does not show a superior and complete knowledge or skill in his field of endeavor.

At the same time missionary work continues to be pioneering work in many areas, and some missionaries still find themselves in situations where they must tackle jobs as best they can, or else the job just will not be done at all.

This combination of circumstances and needs, i.e., increasing specialization and continuing pioneering, creates problems which can hardly be solved without teamwork and cooperation.

We will have to share our specialists with one another. We will have to recognize even more our need to open our institutions and all our works to the scrutiny of specialists of other groups and learn to take their criticism and advice without feeling that they are necessarily hostile when they do criticize. And conversely we will have to encourage our specialists to become not only experts in their fields, but understanding coaches who help the pioneering missionary solve problems which are beyond the extent of his technical training.

Naturally this will produce occasional conflicts between the immediate interests of our own institutions and the common good of wider projects. We will have to be generous and understanding.

The superiors of missionary groups will find their freedom in the assignment and transfer of some of their specialist-subjects curtailed. At times the superiors will have to practice a relatively new type of obedience,

obedience to the exigencies of the common good, obedience to the scientific conclusions of their specialist-consultors.

This whole area is one of challenge to our ability to cooperate intelligently and generously.

CONCLUSION

The missionary spirit is a spirit of love, a reflection of the love that exists within the Trinity, and overflows to mankind. It is a spirit of generosity fearing no sacrifice, in imitation of the Savior, who freely chose immolation for us. The missionary spirit is love of God and neighbor manifested in dedication to the common good of men's souls and bodies. This it seems to me is a pretty good definition of the type of cooperation we have been speaking of as the key to apostolic action.

The missionary spirit is also a spirit of confidence—a conviction that the Holy Spirit speaks to us—and He is speaking to us in the events of the world, the aspirations and frustrations of modern man. The missionary spirit does not fear the world. We will not ignore the world around us. We will dare to accept it as prudently discovered in our studies.

The missionary spirit is the opposite of hedonism. We will not hang on to personal security or status, or excessive material possessions that compromise the apostolate.

The missionary spirit is creative. We will not look for cities nor souls already perfect. Of these we will find none. We will sow the seeds of the Kingdom of God, and cultivate its growth according to the possibilities permitted by God.

The missionary spirit is merciful, and like the Good Shepherd, we will care for sinners. And like redeemed sinners, we ourselves will be humble and accept the help of others.

So that eyes steadfastly upon Christ, and the Body of Christ, we will see the good that is in others, and that good will take root and grow in us.

Ecumenical Aspects of Apostolic Cooperation

John Coventry Smith

It is my intention to share with you some of the thinking which at least a part of the Protestant and Orthodox Churches have been doing within the last ten or fifteen years concerning the mission of the Church, and thereby enable you to understand something of where we are and how we may be related to one another.

The first thing that must be said is that the basic elements of the Christian message remain unchangeable, though the world and the Church change. That which God has done in Jesus Christ on our behalf and on behalf of the whole world is the center and core of our message. But the Church to which this message is committed and the world in which it must be shared are changing radically.

A NEW INTERDEPENDENCE

We live in a new kind of world. It is trite to say that we are at the end of an era in human history, but nevertheless it is true and there is no other concise way to say it. We do live at the end of an era and in this era we are in the midst of changes which mark its end, and are on the verge of participation in a new era.

We have sometimes described the previous era in human history as the age of colonialism. This was a period when, from a base in Europe and then from North America, the countries of the West reached out in discovery, exploration, and colonization into the far corners of the earth. This era is now at an end, and the influence and control of the Western nations is being rolled back politically, militarily, and economically.

William NcNeil, a professor of history at the University of Chicago, in a book published last year called *The Rise of the West*, describes the development across the long centuries by which civilizations have stimulated one another to move in the direction of the *oikumene.* He documents the fact that this movement in history has been accelerated in the last decades until we are about to see the firm establishment of a world civilization based upon the industrial and technological advances that have arisen through the West. Dr. Arend van Leeuwen, a Dutch theologian and historian, in another book published last year called *Christianity in World History*, follows this same thesis but adds the fact that from the Christian standpoint this development in history of movement toward an *oikumene* is of God. This is the way that God has planned it from the beginning. One can see the influence of Christ upon the world in the development of the technological civilization and its establishment among all peoples.

These changes are emphasized in the new appreciation of the interdependence of communities of peoples across the world. The late President Kennedy in 1961, at the Fourth of July celebration in Philadelphia, stated that we must now place alongside of the Declaration of Independence a new Declaration of Interdependence. It is significant also that whereas in 1776, when we sought our independence from Great Britain as a colonial power, we at the same time said that we would have no entangling alliances with any foreign powers. In our time, each of the new nations in Africa that makes its declaration of independence, at the same time is making an application to be a member of the United Nations. This is symbolic of the change that has come in two centuries. I was saying something of this to a group of businessmen in New Rochelle and was explaining how difficult I sometimes found it to communicate what I meant. One of the businessmen interrupted me to say that they did not find it difficult to understand me, for in their businesses they were aware that they must now take into consideration not only the sources of raw material in the whole world, but also the markets of the whole world.

The second emphasis that one must make in the midst of these world changes is that this world civilization, which is rapidly being established, is to be an industrial, technological, and urban civilization. In other words, the megalopolis in which we live here on the Eastern seaboard of the United States is likely to be the forerunner of the kind of civilization that will be established in many other parts of the world and where most of the people of the world will live. As far as our own approach to the problem of the mission of the Church is concerned, this means an understanding of the kind of sociological complexes in which people will live, and of the fact that in a world technological civilization there will be means of communication, across the boundaries of nation and race, such as we have not had in times past.

A NEW CHURCH

So much for the fact that we live in a new kind of world with its implications for the work of the Christian Church. The second aspect which we now face is the fact that we belong to a new kind of Church and that this Church is also affected by the changing world in which we live. Perhaps it is enough to say that during these last centuries the mission agencies of the Church, and the mission societies that have been organized, have been influenced by the kind of historical situation in which they were conceived. I am not being critical of our forefathers. They were adequate for their time, and I hope and pray that we shall be as adequate as they were. Nevertheless, we fail if we do not recognize that they were influenced by the adventure of European and North American peoples as they reached out across the world, and that in many respects they took on the coloration of the colonial period. Perhaps a mission agency can be described legitimately in some of its aspects as being "the colonial office of the Church."

The changes that have come about among Protestant and Orthodox Churches would indicate that there is now emerging a world Christian community that finds expression in the World Council of Churches. This is not a monolithic organization that is controlled from the top down, but it is a group of churches, now numbering more than 200, that find in this organization a means of expressing their unity in Jesus Christ. They do compose one expression of the world Christian community that now exists in the interdependent community of peoples.

In the same sense Vatican II can be interpreted as expressing in the Roman Catholic Church something of the result of the same impact. One of my Roman Catholic friends has described one of the purposes of Vatican II as the "internationalization of the Church." In other words, he also is saying that one of its purposes is to more adequately express the nature of the Roman Catholic Church as a world Christian community.

We in the Protestant and Roman Catholic Churches are likely to think that this is confined to our own experience. We know that God has been speaking to us and continues to speak, both through the Scriptures and through the events of history. It has been something of a surprise to me in the last four or five years to discover that outside of those who are associated with either the historic Protestant or Roman Catholic Churches, something of the same thing is happening in other Christian circles. We have had conversations at times with leaders of the independent missions, people whom we sometimes regard as on the fringes of the Christian movement, though they have a deep concern with the missionary activity of the Church. I have discovered that they also are feeling the impact of what God is saying to us in our time. You will be interested in knowing that in a recent consultation, lasting two or three days, leaders of the independent missionary organizations also were eager to talk about relationships with the Roman Catholic Church. We had supposed that this might be a further cause of estrangement between us. We discovered that our common concern at this point was a means of drawing us closer together.

To sum up, we must say that there has been emerging in our time an understanding that God is leading us, through the Holy Spirit, to a greater appreciation of the unity, and integrity, and wholeness of the Church as a world Christian community and the necessity for this wholeness to be part of the witness of the Church to a world community of peoples.

Let me now talk about the special relationships between Roman Catholics and Protestants. I do not mean to exhaust the subject, for we will be talking about this in many conferences in these days that lie ahead. Nevertheless before we talk about some of the directions for mission which face us in these days immediately ahead, let us comment upon one or two aspects of the relationships between Roman Catholics and Protestants.

I am not a theological expert, but my own conclusions are something like this. The growing appreciation of one another that we find in Protestant and Roman Catholic circles does not depend upon compromise of doctrinal principles. We do not expect that anyone will change his convictions because he has come to respect other people who hold different convictions as being Christian also. There will be no compromise on doctrine, at least no radical changes of doctrinal position. The rifts between us will remain and they are deep.

But what has happened is that we have come to understand that in this new kind of world we are bound together within the Body of Christ and must respect one another as Christians. Not only must we respect from a distance, but we must take into consideration the viewpoints of others as we make our plans. In fact, if possible our plans should take into consideration the plans that are being made by other parts of the Body of Christ.

Bishop Leslie Newbigin, who is the outstanding leader of Protestant and Orthodox missionary work, having been for the last five years director of the Division of World Mission and Evangelism of the World Council of Churches, and recently named Bishop of Madras of the Church of South India, has put it this way when he spoke to groups both in Europe and North America. He says that for the next decade at least and possibly longer the most important single element in the background of our thinking as Protestants must be this relationship with the Roman Catholic Church. Dr. D. T. Niles, a leader of the church in Ceylon and himself a Ceylonese, has put it in a slightly different form when he recalls that for the last several years he has been trying to interest an Anglican bishop in Ceylon in cooperation and the Anglican bishop has consistently refused. Finally when Dr. Niles went to see him once again, the Anglican bishop asked him, "Don't you see that you make no progress by asking for cooperation? My position is clear." And Dr. Niles replied, "God won't let me let you alone." We live in the kind of world where we cannot any longer let each other alone. We have to try to understand one another and try to know what God is saying to each of us and together about the mission of His Church in the world.

I personally appreciate the fact that at the World Council and Vatican level we already have committees that are discussing our common Christian mission. We now have at the National Council level a committee that is working with Bishop Carberry's committee and talking about various ways of consulting together. And in some of the Protestant denominations something of this same thing is happening. We in the United Presbyterian Church in the U.S.A., for example, have a committee which is working in the fullest cooperation with a committee under the chairmanship of Bishop Ernest Unterkoefler, which had its first meeting in Washington, D.C., July 27, 1965. The theme for our discussion is likely to be "The Work of the Holy Spirit in the Renewal and Reform of the Church." This is a good Roman Catholic theme and a good Presbyterian theme.

CHURCH AND MISSION: ONE

Let us now look at some of the things which we have been considering during the last ten or fifteen years concerning the mission of the Church. There is an appreciation of the fact that mission is the obligation of the whole Church. I remember attending the Assembly of the World Council of Churches at Evanston in 1954, and listening to the program one evening when the mission of the Church in its world-wide aspects was presented. Two of us walked out after the meeting was over and commented that "we had missed the boat." By that we meant that we were still speaking in terms of mission being the extension of the work of Western churches into the life of the whole world. We had failed to understand that when approximately 160 or 170 churches across the world came together in a world assembly that there was a new aspect of the wholeness of the Christian community and its responsibilities for the whole world. At New Delhi, in 1961, at the Third Assembly of the World Council we were ready at least to express it in sharper terms. We expressed it by saying that the responsibility of the Church now was not for three continents, but for six. The meaning of this arises from the fact that at least in Protestant circles missionary concern has been for Asia, Africa, and Latin America and from the base of Europe and North America. Now we understand that all of the churches together in the Christian community have a concern for the whole world and therefore for all six continents. There can be no "mission continents." There can really be no "mission areas." Even in the United States we have regarded areas of life as being of particular concern to missionary societies: Negro communities, Indian communities, communities in what we call "the inner-city." We have found it difficult to justify some of our terminology in this new context. We are continually reminding ourselves that we ought not to call churches by the terms "older" or "younger." Some of the so-called "younger" churches are now more than 100 years old and hardly qualify as young children. I think this may also apply to your own use of the term "needy churches." There is a sense in which all of us are needy churches, in need of what God says to all of us through our sister churches.

We are also increasingly aware that the mission is for the whole Church, that each community of believers has a missionary responsibility. We had an Advisory Study Committee in the United Presbyterian Church to look at the work of the Church outside the bounds of the United States. It came back to us with a 96-page document of recommendations, but the core of it clustered around the statement, "Each community of believers has a right to expect the gifts of the Spirit, which if recognized, trained, and used, are adequate for the witness of the Church at that time and place and to the ends of the earth." We have too long assumed that there was a kind of halo around the missionary society of the West and that therefore when a church was established in a given area the missionary society continued to carry the responsibility of mission. At least I know it is a Protestant heresy that the Church and the mission are separate. Now we are understanding that each Christian community must in fact be a missionary community. This means, of course, that there may be missionaries from all of these churches that have been established around the world. I remember talking about this with groups of Christians in Bangkok in 1956, and a young pastor from Singapore who was present spoke up and said, "You mean we could be missionaries? I thought this was an American monopoly." I am not sure that he was entirely innocent in his question, for he was standing beside his own bishop, who was an American, and he wanted his bishop to hear what he said. Nevertheless, this idea of missionaries coming from the so-called younger churches has advanced to such an extent that by now more than 200 missionaries from the churches in Asia are working outside the bounds of their own geographical area.

The remarks above are documented by Johannes Blauw in *The Missionary Nature of the Church.* Here he denies that there is any such thing as a theology of mission. There is only Christian theology which is missionary by its very nature. Dr. D. T. Niles has a book called *Upon the Earth,* which in a more popular manner emphasizes the same theme. In the World Council of Churches the Study Department has been working on what it calls "A Quest for Missionary Structures of Congregations." And this has had its influence in many parts of the world.

We have been led, therefore, to emphasize mission as the very essence of the Church and at the center of the Church's concern. I have been interested in noting that Roman Catholics are also raising questions that grow out of the implications of this emphasis, for you are saying that if the mission of the Church belongs to the Church, then what is the real place of the missionary societies? In a similar way we have been asking these same questions and we are very much aware that the missionary societies have been drawn much closer into the life of the Church. This is true in my own denomination, where the Boards of Foreign Missions have been replaced by a Commission on Ecumenical Mission and Relations. Our missionary activity outside the United States is now part of the concern of a Commission which has to do with the relations of the Church to the whole of the world Christian community. In the National Council of Churches in a similar manner the Division of Foreign Missions has become the Division of Overseas Ministries. It is also much closer to the center of the National Council of Churches; at least we in the Division of Overseas Ministries find ourselves participating in the life of the National Council in a way that was not possible or even considered in the past. The International Missionary Council, which was separate from the World Council of Churches, has now become the Division of World Mission and Evangelism of the World Council and finds itself participating in the whole life of the World Council.

This means also that mission and service are more closely affliliated. In some of our churches the service agencies and the foreign-mission agencies have been combined. This also is true at the National Council level. Moreover, we find ourselves much more closely associated with those in the Church who are concerned with Church and society. One of the people who attended the conferences between the World Council and the Vatican concerning the mission of the Church and then concerning Church and society, said that he felt that the affinity between the people who worked together in Church and society and the people who worked together in the missionary activity of the Church was greater than that which bound them together within the Protestant or Roman Catholic Churches. However, this is changing. Missionaries on furlough find themselves involved in the civil-rights movement here in the United States and discover that their concern with society is a part of their missionary commitment.

This all has theological implications. What we have

been engaged in now leads us to consider in the whole Church some of the impact that must be made upon the theological thinking of the Church. In the World Council of Churches, for example, between the Third Assembly at New Delhi and the next Assembly in 1968, the Church has been challenged to study the theme "The Finality of Jesus Christ in an Age of Universal History." This obviously arises from a concern of the Church for mission in the world. We are also being challenged to study the meaning of "secularism" and more recently the issue of "conversion." This was a theme at the Central Committee meeting of the World Council in Enugu, Nigeria, January 1965, and it is also the general theme for study by the National Council of Churches and by Bishop Carberry's committee in the joint consideration of Roman Catholic and Protestant affairs.

EMERGING REGIONALISM

There is still another emphasis that has arisen in the last fifteen years among the Protestant and Orthodox Churches that will be of considerable interest to you. We find that there has been an emerging regionalism among the churches. In Asia we now have the East Asia Christian Conference and more recently an All Africa Church Conference has been organized. They are semi-independent but for the most part are composed of the same churches that are members of the World Council of Churches. This regionalism has arisen because so-called "younger" churches have felt that when they went to the world gatherings they were still a small minority and sometimes not equipped to participate in the consultations that were dominated by the people of the West. They therefore sought some place that was closer home, not so far away, not "high up in the sky." Here they were able to consider the problems that were common to them and to learn from one another. This was resisted by the ecumenical organizations at the beginning. I remember Dr. Visser 't Hooft raising the question when the East Asia Christian Conference was being organized and saying, "Does this mean that you will not knock at the door in Geneva?" The obvious answer, of course, was that once having consulted together they would knock at the door in Geneva more insistently, and such has been the case.

It is quite evident that if we are to associate one with another either in the World Council or across the lines between Protestants and Roman Catholics, it must be with the expectation that we have something to learn from one another. At my second meeting of the Central Committee of the World Council in Rochester, New York, in 1963, I discovered that the Executive Committee had asked Dr. Visser 't Hooft, the General Secretary of the World Council, to prepare an address on the theme "What Does it Mean to be a Member of the World Council?" I supposed that this was a rather innocuous subject. But as he developed it I soon discovered that he was dealing with the very purposes of the Council itself and the practices of the Council as these had been expressed in the experience of its meetings. His conclusion was that memership in the Council inevitably meant that each member was willing to listen and if necessary to modify its viewpoint as the result of discussion. One of the older members of the Central Committee was on his feet as soon as Dr. Visser 't Hooft concluded, to say that if his church had understood that this was the meaning of membership in the World Council they would not have joined. He was quite sure that his church was not aware of his being present at the meeting of the Central Committee and he did not intend to make any report to them. We can laugh at this, but I think it is true that we do not report back to our churches as we ought concerning experiences that we have of an ecumenical character.

We have recently had an experience in the United States that illustrates what Dr. Visser 't Hooft was saying. The National Council of Churches has been concerned during these last six or eight months about the situation in Vietnam. It made a statement in February 1965 and then in June, at its General Board, but it did not take very seriously its responsibility in this regard until it was reminded by Dr. Visser 't Hooft's visit in June 1965, then by a communication from the East Asia Christian Conference, and finally by a visit of five members of the Japanese Christian community, who had come to tell us what American participation in Vietnam looked like to Christians in Asia. I am not saying that we must agree completely with what people outside the United States say about us, but what I am saying is that within the Christian community we must be willing to listen to what God is saying to us through the whole community and if necessary to modify, under the guidance of the Holy Spirit, the viewpoints that we have held in the past.

Now let me list rather rapidly some practical ecumenical approaches that we have found stimulating in Protestant missions. We are very much aware that there must be joint planning. You will be surprised to discover that there has never been a full world survey by Protestant and Orthodox Churches of what they have been doing across the world. This has begun now under the impetus of the meeting in Mexico City, in December 1963, of the Commission on World Mission and Evangelism. The first survey has been completed in West Africa and some surprising opportunities have been opened up as a result of it.

We have also been engaged in what we call Joint Action for Mission. Perhaps I ought to say that we have been engaged in studying it, we are not yet very fully involved in such joint action. The term is used to describe concentrations of activity in a limited geographical area by all the Christian forces in the area as they study the needs and the resources that are available. This does not mean a unified approach, but a coordinated one in which each group with its resources is assigned a specific task within the total plan and often without hope of "denominational dividends."

We also have discovered that at the world level there is a growing necessity for the need of "interchurch aid." For example, we now have a program for the next five years in the World Council to secure support to the extent of a minimum of ten million dollars for assistance to churches in Africa. This will be done regardless of denominational relationship. No one mission agency or even a small group of mission agencies could be responsible for such an approach. This does not take the place of the relationships of mission agencies, but is in addition to their efforts, so that there may be an overall look and an overall means of assisting those that are in the most significant areas.

In a similar way there has been established a Theological Education Fund toward which 35 churches across the world contribute. Under a competent committee, decisions are made in regard to aiding theological seminaries in the education of ministers and pastors. This is done on the basis of expert study and in order to help the most significant areas regardless of denominational relationship. My own church made a gift of half a million dollars for the first five years and promised another half million for the second five years of the Fund. We have no way of knowing what proportion of this will go to Presbyterian-related theological seminaries. We are now extending this to a Christian Literature Fund and we are studying whether or not this has implications for our approaches to the work of Christian higher education and to medical work.

One practical approach which has been suggested by the Mexico City meeting, but has not yet been implemented, is that we should seek in the next five years to establish every missionary community as "interracial, interdenominational, and international." Obviously this was an attempt to express within the Body of Christ the meaning of our being one in Christ before the whole world. No missionary group should by its nature even unconsciously teach people that the Christian faith belongs to a particular confession, or to a particular racial group, or to a particular nationality.

The interpretation of this to the church from which we come is one of the great responsibilities that you and I share. If the church is to participate, then it must understand its very nature and why it is called upon to participate. Paul and Barnabas were not only the first missionaries, they were the first interpreters. Second only to what they did on the first missionary journey was their report back to the Church at Antioch and then to the Council at Jerusalem. This changed the nature of the Christian community as it approached the world. Incidentally, their interpretation recruited a new missionary, Silas, who was to be Paul's companion on the second journey.

The role of interpreting the nature of the Church is a responsible one. It is one that the Church has come to respect highly in our time because together we are dealing with our responsibilities unto God to take the message He has given us in Jesus Christ and to share it with all mankind.

Some Missiological Reflections on Current Theology

Ronan Hoffman, O.F.M. Conv.

Only in recent years have we spoken of a "missionary Church" in reference to the entire Church and not merely that minority part of it really active in the missionary movement. The notion of a "missionary Church," however, is in need of much development. It is possible to think of it as one in which all church members play an increasingly larger role in the mission apostolate as we know it today. This appears to be a too simplistic view, although it must be admitted that discussion of it is still insufficiently mature to be able to determine it precisely.

For several decades Protestant and Catholic theologians and missiologists have been seeking to clarify the concepts of both "church" and "mission." The Second Vatican Council has given us fresh insights into the Catholic understanding of both these concepts, although the practical ramifications of these insights may not be known for another half-century. Only when we completely understand both "church" and "mission" in their full extent will we understand what a "missionary Church" is or ought to be.

At present we are witnessing various shifts of thought in theology which are destined to influence the mission movement for years to come. These shifts in thought, no matter how small or insignificant they may appear to some, can have far-reaching consequences. It will be possible here only to note some new emphases in theology together with some reflections, altogether too abbreviated, on their implication for the mission movement. Some of these emphases are:

1. The shift from considering the Church as an independent entity to Christ, the Founder of the Church.

2. Decentralization in Church government, which necessarily involves the hierarchy in the mission apostolate.

3. Greater emphasis upon the need of serving the world instead of the world serving the Church.

4. A moving away from the mission apostolate considered as a conquest for souls to the idea of dialogue with non-Christians.

5. Substitution of an attitude of competition with other Christians for one of sincere dialogue with them in the field of religion and collaboration with them in the field of social action.

6. Rediscovery of the notion of eschatology.

7. Admission of the diaspora situation of Christianity.

One of the most significant of these for understanding "mission" in the future lies in the understanding and acceptance of the diaspora situation of Christians. As Karl Rahner has pointed out, we have to admit that, although Christianity exists everywhere in the world (though in varying proportions), it also exists everywhere as a diaspora. It is effectually, in terms of numbers, a minority everywhere. "Indeed," he writes, "we are undoubtedly in an era which is going to see an increase in this diaspora character, no matter what causes we may assign to it."[1]

Rahner then goes on to say that our diaspora situation is not merely a fact to be recognized *a posteriori* and with dismay. It is something which, on the basis of our faith, we should have expected, in the sense of a "must" within the history of salvation. Difficult though it may be to accept from a human point of view, we must remember that Christ promised to His Church "not only that she would endure until the end of time but, just as clearly, that His work would always be a sign of contradiction and persecution, of dire and . . . desperate combat; . . . that the victory of Christianity would not be the fruit of immanent development and widening and a steady, progressive leaving of the world, but would come as the act of God coming in judgment to gather up world history into its wholly unpredictable and unexpected end."[2]

We must stress that our diaspora situation is not just a fact but a "must" in the history of salvation, even as the passion and death of Christ was a "must." This means that we cannot simply approve of either as something justified in advance. But just as Christ's death on the cross must be accepted by us as necessary

[1] Karl Rahner, S.J., *The Christian Commitment* (New York, Sheed and Ward, 1963), p. 17. For what follows see the whole of Chapter I, "The Present Situation of Christians: a Theological Interpretation of the Position of Christians in the Modern World."
[2] *Ibid.*, pp. 18-19.

in the mysterious design of God for man's redemption and salvation, so too we must accept with the eyes of faith our diaspora situation. Despite the fact that the modern Christian mission movement is greater than ever before in the history of the Church, we Christians together do not account for much more than one-fourth of the human race. We are a minority group and destined to become even smaller in a more rapidly growing non-Christian world. In spite of all our efforts, the proportion of Catholics in the total world population rose between 1880-1958 by only 0.14 per cent. Rather than becoming disheartened by such figures, we should rather ask what the Lord of history is trying to tell us through them.

It would be wrong to conclude, because the Church is but the *pusillus grex* and intended by the Lord to be such, that we can cease to be missionary. Such a conclusion is absolutely unwarranted. On the contrary, we have to want the number of Christians to increase, to want their influence and their importance to grow. We must want the concrete realization of a Christian spirit in public affairs and social institutions to increase. We must work for this. But, despite all this, our growing diaspora situation is something to be expected, something foretold in Scripture, something we can count on, *and which need not cause us any inner conflict or missionary defeatism.*

In the modern mission movement our methodology was too often based on the politics of colonization rather than the solid base of Scripture. For example, due to thinking of the Kingdom of Christ after the manner of the kingdom of Spain, it was thought that, just as every Indian in the New World had to become a subject of his majesty, the Catholic king, so too every Indian *had* to become a subject of the Vicar of Christ. Such a view, fundamental to the missionary methodology in the colonizing period (and which has prevailed up to the present day in Latin America) cannot be supported by the Bible or tradition. That God ought to have the 100 per cent is easily understood; that *we* must have the 100 per cent is another matter. It is very important that our image of the Church be that of Christ, not that of man. We are to be the "leaven in the mass," not the mass of mankind. Recall St. Augustine's saying: "Many whom God has, the Church does not have; and many whom the Church has, God does not have."

On the other hand, the Church has a universal vocation. It is, in the words of Vatican II, the "universal sacrament of salvation" (*De Ecclesia,* No. 48). This is fraught with missionary meaning. Even though the Church is destined to be the *pusillus grex* of the Gospel, nonetheless it is the sign of salvation for all mankind. God wills that all men be saved, and it is through the work of the Church that this comes about. *Extra ecclesiam nulla salus* still retains its meaning, yet it must be understood more optimistically and in a less restrictive manner than it was by some theologians of the past.

The Church has always taught what is repeated in the Constitution on the Church: "Those also can attain to salvation who through no fault of their own do not know the Gospel of Christ or His Church, yet sincerely seek God and moved by grace strive by their deeds to do His will as it is known to them through the dictates of conscience. Nor does Divine Providence deny the helps necessary for salvation to those who, without blame on their part, have not yet arrived at an explicit knowledge of God and with His grace strive to live a good life" (*De Ecclesia,* No. 16). The redemption of Christ is universal and the grace of Christ has been at work everywhere in the world, even where the Church and her missionaries have not reached.

MISSIONARY BY NATURE

Still, because the Church is the sacrament of salvation of the whole world, it must foster the missions with care and attention. The community of those who explicitly believe in Christ is used by Him as an instrument for the salvation of all, and is sent forth into the whole world to teach all nations and to preach the Gospel to every creature. In other words, the Church is essentially missionary by divine constitution. The concrete forms whereby the Church carries out her missionary task, however, vary from age to age. It is our task to discover how the Church can best do this in our age.

Current ecclesiology requires that we place numbers and quantitative growth in the background rather than considering these as the criterion of "success," as we have been, and still are, wont to do. In the past we have wrongly conceived the mission task in terms of converting as many as possible, overlooking the fact that our Lord commanded the Apostles to *teach* all nations, not to *convert* them. The first is possible for human beings, not so the second. Faith is a gift of God, and God alone decides to whom He will give it: Paul plants, Apollos waters, but *God* gives the increase. The mission is to teach, not to convert, even though hoping that God may bring many into His Church.

PURPOSE OF MISSIONS

For several centuries up to the present one, the goal of missionary work was generally considered to be twofold: the propagation of the faith and the salvation of souls. An important advance was made in this century when we rephrased this purpose in terms of the establishment of the Church. Now we find a further change from the image of a social institution to the Church considered as the sign and instrument of the universal salvation of Christ.

This shift is of great significance for the mission apostolate. Despite the value of the formula, "the establishment of the Church," it had one serious weakness which was not immediately evident but which can be seen more clearly today. This formula laid stress upon the establishment of the visible Church through such institutions as churches, schools, hospitals, etc. In so doing, we have become the victims of "institutionalism" to the point where upkeep and administration of these institutions in many places seriously interferes with the task of evangelism. Today, therefore, it is necessary for us to rid ourselves of the excessively juridical concept of a visible, institutionalized Church and consider it rather as the "people of God," as that community of believers who are in this world the sign and instrument of salvation for all mankind. We have placed too much emphasis on the construction of buildings, too little on the liturgy and other religious means to be used in forming the people of God.

In 1961, the Bishops' Conference of the Congo made an important decision. They determined to stop building all pastoral work on institutions and to develop an apostolate for an effective presence in the world; to concentrate apostolic efforts on the creation of living Christian communities by preaching the Gospel, making full use of the liturgy, training the laity, undertaking charitable works; to decrease as much as possible the burden of the Church's institutions; and to put the existing institutions completely at the service of the community; to collaborate sincerely and wholeheartedly with non-Catholics for the building of a world that is more just and dedicated to human welfare. These bishops of Africa seem aware that the Church (like Christ) is in this world to die, not to erect institutions or power structures which would prevent any form of crucifixion. Here is a far better understanding of the "mission" than has been manifested in many parts of the United States.

We in the United States and Europe could profit a great deal by interchanging personnel not only from our countries to mission lands, but vice versa. Here is a form of interchange which for years Protestants have found of great value, yet one which we Catholics have hardly even considered.

As stated previously, current theological shifts of thought require that we eradicate all vestiges of the attitude and spirit which conceives of the mission as a crusade of conquest, setting out to conquer peoples (or worse, "souls"), imposing on them Western cultural and ecclesiastical forms. Rather, mission must be viewed in terms of witness and service—loving, disinterested service. A part of this service, of course, must include the offering of the Christian message, yet withal avoiding all kinds of proselytism.

In place of conquest we must set "dialogue," the term used by Paul VI in *Ecclesiam Suam* to describe the mission today. On the one hand, it is a dialogue of salvation, as we have always been deeply aware, but which we must understand today in a more profound sense. It is principally a dialogue of salvation, in which our mission is to offer the message of Christ's redemption and salvation to all men for their free acceptance or rejection, granting to them that same freedom in religious matters that God Himself gives to all men.

We must take the initiative in this dialogue, as well as in "the other dialogue"—the dialogue with the modern world, by serving it and working with all others to help solve the problems of mankind today. The forms of this dialogue are many and varied, ranging from such problems as world poverty and hunger to seeking a deeper understanding with all men, seeking wider areas of cooperation, discovering a truer sense of brotherhood and solidarity with humanity, searching for ways of justice and world peace, and so on.

UNDERSTANDING MISSION

The concept of "dialogue" is of great value for a clearer and more penetrating understanding of "mission," for it implies at least in a general way both the goals to be sought and the manner of seeking these goals. Compare, for example, the fifteenth-century outlook and attitude of the Church toward non-Christians with those of our day. Pope Innocent VIII wrote in 1486 that he considered as his chief concern "the propagation of the orthodox faith, the increase of the Christian religion, the salvation of barbarian nations, and the repression of infidels and their conversion to the faith." The expression is typical of the popes of that age.

In 1964 Cardinal Marella, the President of the newly formed Secretariat for Non-Christian Religions, stated in a press conference shortly after his appointment: "The present time calls for a new contact between the Church and non-Christians—a contact of sympathy and mutual understanding, based on study but also on frankness and the rejection of every prejudice. This will lead to mutual esteem, to a sincere *rapprochement*, and to cordial collaboration in all possible fields, for example, in defending the religious idea which is being attacked by atheistic materialism."

Today, more than ever before, it is necessary to create a climate of understanding by a true mutual knowledge. The new Secretariat is not another Propaganda, it will not engage in proselytism. Rather, in the words of Cardinal Marella, "We shall make known the Catholic Church, and we will in turn learn to know the non-Christian religions."

It is for us to understand how we not only can but *must* be missionary and ecumenical—both with our fellow Christians and with non-Christians—at one and the same time. Both attitudes are united in the idea of "dialogue." In the future the manner, the methods, the attitudes, the reasons for entering into dialogue with others will differ sharply from those of the past.

For several decades both Catholic and Protestant missiologists have been trying to clarify the idea of "mission." That the concept has not yet been clarified to the point of universal acceptance in Catholic circles could be seen in the inability of the Commission on the Missions to agree on the definition of "mission" in the third session of the Council. The problem is not merely semantic, for many practical consequences follow on the meaning attached to it.

LATIN AMERICA

This point must be stressed, because the mission apostolate of the past four centuries has proceeded according to the theology developed after the Council of Trent, and we are still proceeding in our mission work to too large an extent according to that outdated theology. This may well be true especially in Latin America today. Remember that the Pontifical Commission for Latin America was set up in 1958, at a time when theological views widely accepted today had not yet reached Rome, where the planning for the Latin American *anschluss* was done.

Since theological views have changed so rapidly and so radically since 1958, it is necessary to ask whether the apostolic work being undertaken there by European and North American personnel is "missionary," recalling that, traditionally, missionary work has been understood as those apostolic efforts directed to non-Christians *outside* the Church.*

If we answer that the work there is not "missionary" in that sense, then we must honestly and courageously ask whether, under the influence of an outdated theology, we are merely trying desperately to retain mere numbers on the Church's roll there, unconsciously overlooking the fact that at times we honestly admit that the Church is in the diaspora situation even in Latin America?

On the other hand, if we should answer that it *is* "missionary" work, then why do we say that there is a need for more than 150,000 priests there, as has been stated many times? That "need" is based on the assumption that the large majority of Latin Americans are practicing Catholics and that every 1,000 practicing Catholics require the services of a priest. But if most are not practicing Catholics—and no one seriously contends that they are—then the "need" for 150,000 more priests diminishes substantially. But if one still persists that there is such a "need," then why do we not project a similar "need" for priests in other parts of the world where the apostolic work is without question missionary? But if, mesmerized by numbers, we were to try to project such "needs," we would find ourselves in the very uncomfortable position of putting burdens on ourselves which, humanly speaking, we are simply incapable of fulfilling. And certainly God does not expect the impossible from us.

* [Ed. Note: The Decree on the Missionary Activity of the Church states that traditional missionary work "should also furnish help to those churches, founded long since, which are in a certain state of regression or weakness." (No. 19).]

Is the gigantic effort to "save" the Church in Latin America distracting us from the real mission—the dialogue with the non-Christian peoples of Africa and Asia, who incidentally make up the greater part of mankind? Are we in effect, apart from good intentions, unconsciously yet really trying to defend the last remnant of "sociological Catholicism," or even of "ghetto Catholicism," thus making ourselves less missionary in the sense of taking the message of salvation to the *whole* world?

We can see things clearly in regard to certain areas, but perhaps not in regard to others. For instance, if an individual parish or diocese or nation were to insist that the unit should tighten its forces and concentrate on missionary work *inside* its borders, would we not rightly accuse it of being nonmissionary, even of being antimissionary? This in fact actually happened in postwar France, where the number of missionary vocations and departures diminished as a result of insistence that greater "missionary" efforts had to be exerted *within* the country. We must dare to be honest in looking at our present apostolic efforts in Latin America. Are we trying to retain there *our* image of the Kingdom of God on earth, or striving to realize the true Kingdom of Christ everywhere?

Recall the Old Christians of Japan. They *preserved* their form of Christianity for two and one-half centuries. But they merely preserved it. In the process their form of Christianity became decadent, corrupt—and nonmissionary.

This is not to say that Europe and North America should not be concerned about the needs of the Church in Latin America. It does mean that the Church in all these regions, including Latin America, must be concerned about the missionary needs in Africa and Asia. Much attention has been given to the needs of the Church in Latin America, but much less notice has been given to the needs of the Church in these other two continents. Is it not peculiar, to say the least, that there is a Papal Commission for Latin America, yet nothing similar for Africa and Asia? Have we lost—at least temporarily—our universal vision and vocation? It is important to determine whether our efforts in Latin America are truly "missionary," or whether they are serving to distract us from the mission *ad extra,* the mission to the non-Christian world.

THE FUTURE

In what direction should our future striving be? To try to mount an ever-increasing massive effort to seek conversions through mass Baptism where this is still possible; to seek influence and power and prestige through visible institutions; to call upon Catholics in Europe and North America to collaborate in a last-ditch stand to protect "sociological Catholicism" in the Latin American continent at the expense possibly of losing our universal vocation?

Or should we aim at a better biblical understanding of the mission of Christ and His Church, accepting through the eyes of faith and hope the factual diaspora situation in which we find ourselves, without being disturbed about our size or the number of our institutions but rather leaving these things entirely to God;

and set out in a more energetic manner, with a universal outlook, to take the initiative in a dialogue with men everywhere? As noted previously, we should not be preoccupied with numbers of conversions, since this is not within our power. Let us rather address ourselves to the task of witnessing, preaching, serving mankind—and leave it completely to God whether "success" follows or not.

It seems that for some time in the future we should look forward to "missionary progress" *within* the Church rather than outside it. It should consist not so much in quantitative growth in membership but rather in a qualitative growth within the members of the Church. It should consist in three things: (1) a greater awareness of the nature of the Church and its mission in the modern world; (2) a continual renewal and reform of the Church and its members; and (3) a carrying out of the mission to non-Christians in the form of dialogue in place of proselytism.

In order to achieve this type of "missionary progress," much is required of all of us. It means that we are going to have to seek the answers to some difficult, yet important, questions.

The more impatient would no doubt like concrete answers to these questions. But this is not possible now. The conciliar commission on the missions could not even agree during the third session on a suitable definition of "mission" and "missionary." Just as we are on the threshold of a new understanding of the nature of the Church, so too we are just at the beginning of a deeper understanding of the mission of the Church. But this understanding cannot be rushed, it must be a gradual process within the members of the Church. The Church will be renewed and reformed, will modify its external institutions and its approach to the apostolate, only through the internal renewal and reform of each of her members.

It is simply impossible at this stage to determine what concrete forms the emphases in current ecclesiology will have upon the future of the mission. For example, it is impossible at the moment to predict what the collegiality of the bishops will mean for the mission apostolate in years to come. That should not even be our concern at present. Rather, we should all concern ourselves with the task of steeping ourselves in the total view of the Church as it has been presented to us by the Council, replacing our excessively canonical concepts of the past by more theological ones. It is not yet time to devise new organizations, to modify existing ones, to search for new methods. These will no doubt come in their own good time.

Perhaps such a statement is less satisfying than concrete proposals for change. But we need to remind ourselves that the Church is the Church of Christ, and the mission is His, not ours. As Karl Rahner has wisely pointed out:

> The Church entrusts itself to history; it cannot and will not be reconstructed according to the abstract schemes or blueprints of theologians, clerical politicians, journalists, and impatient theorists. . . . It does not know its own earthly future but pursues its pilgrim way, guided by the incomprehensible

God as the guide of humanity into the mystery of God.[3]

Mystery—the Church is a mystery, a sacrament. Yet the Church knows that it is sacrament, not for its own salvation, but for that of the whole world. Consequently, it must ever remain true to its missionary character, as that character is made ever more clear to it by the Holy Spirit.

[3] Karl Rahner, S.J., "The Christian of the Future," Vol. 2, *Herder Correspondence* (July 1965), p. 232.

Redeemed and Redemptive

JAMES M. DARBY, S.M.

I have been called upon to present methods for inculcating the apostolic spirit in our schools in the missions. My basic strategy in answering the call may seem to be to avoid the subject. However, this is not my intention. Neither is it to attempt to concentrate on methodology and certainly not on *inculcating*, of all things, apostolic spirit, which as far as my own limited experience bears out, responds to method like the cowlick to the comb.

There are, of course, conditions conducive to infusing the dimension of Catholicity into our schools and, for that matter, into any apostolic endeavor of the Church. One could argue, I suppose, that such conditions are automatically subsumed in any discussion, such as this, of method. However, given the times in which we find ourselves, my personal reaction, arrived at after careful consideration, some fairly heavy reading, and a little consultation, is to adopt the following program for procedure:

1. I am going to define the position of the missionary in the Church, so that we can see what is expected of him, and even more to the point, what is not.

2. I am going to shine the light of these expectations onto selected areas of the current dialogue about the apostolate of the Church, especially the apostolate of teaching in the schools.

3. I am going to suggest a few ways in which the Catholic teacher responds to his vocation in the Church of Vatican II.

REDEEMED AND REDEMPTIVE EQUALS MISSIONARY

Today, in an attempt to force our insight a bit, the theologian tells us it is the Church that is missionary; *not* the missioner, but the *Church.* Thus he aims at putting each one of us in his proper place, a risky business amidst the burning fevers of personalism. There is more involved here than a point of view, of course; and no one is being downgraded personally by the nuance of the distinction; quite the contrary. What we are being told is that we are, indeed, all missionaries, apostles of the Word, but precisely only insofar as we are Church, the people of God, baptized into and living Christ. That is the point and it is a sound one. Nurtured at the Eucharistic Banquet, the center of the Church's life, we share in the very life of God and, formed by His Word, we only then dare to say, "Thy kingdom come . . . on earth . . . as in heaven."

Thus the redeemed are redemptive; the people of God are in the mission—or they are nothing. Their every activity must be the Church living and giving a fruitful, formative missionary presence; Christ raised aloft drawing all things to Himself. It is the spread of His Kingdom or it is nothing. As the Liturgy of the

Word and the Eucharist binds together heaven and earth for us in an eternal present, so the initiated person, whoever and wherever he is, exists as one in the act of spreading that Word and of sharing that love; his life and all that fills it continues the liturgy, as it were, by incarnating the message and the love of God. In this sense we are all missionaries, we are Church, the people of God, Christ leavening the world.

Failing this, we cannot expect to infuse or create the dimension of Catholicity anywhere, no matter what our work may be. We cannot hope to announce the Kingdom effectively to anyone. There will be no real and lasting results. We may stir up a few things, perhaps some heat over statistics or some unripe commitments that spell plain trouble abroad. A quality job, however, will not get done, simply because the one essential challenge, the purely missionary one, that of being Church, goes ignored and unanswered. Instead, too much self, too much of the merely temporal and the profane, is featured in one's actual living out of his life. He may offer a variety of kinds of witness, but there is no really redemptive effect. Despite what is often good practical knowledge and noteworthy natural virtue, the individual has no sense of the sacredness of his labors, of their being, for example, a participation in the creative work of God; and slowly but inevitably he seems to surrender the whole of his interior life to the unredeemed rhythms of the world, where universal hedonism appears imminent, and economy, the law, and politics generally recognize no God.

The chief ouster of evil is goodness. Desecration of life and its context must give way to consecration, and not by proclamation alone but in every deed and truth. The authentic missioner who is Church is equally committed to his temporal and his eternal vocations. While in quest of happiness in the world beyond, he goes about the construction of the Kingdom of God, in whatever position he is in, through the consecration and dedication of himself and of his whole life, of the social structures and institutions everywhere established and shared by him and, finally, of the world itself. For, in essence, missioner is synonymous with saint, and the essential attitude and work of the Church shines forth in the concrete reality which he is.

As modern theologians are helping us to appreciate more and more, the pre-eminent example of everything that the missioner is called upon to be as Church is the Virgin Mary and, in the light of what we have been saying, the fresh, creative stress today being given to devotion to her is readily understandable. She is the archetype of the Church.

> "Mary also personifies the holiness of the Church. She is the germ-cell of the Church. She carries within her the Church's entire holiness to impart it to the Church assembled. She is the pre-existing Church; she is prior to all the saints and to individual members of the Church. Mary is also the idea of the Church, the idea brought into existence in redeemed and co-redeeming humanity . . . In Mary . . . the Church affirms Her own holy, co-redemptive and redeemed essence. She gratefully recognizes in Mary Her own self in origin and beginning." [1]

[1] Otto Semmelroth, S.J., *Mary, the Archetype of the Church* (New York, Sheed and Ward, 1963), pp. 173-74.

Her presence to us is *Church;* she is for us a formative and redeeming existential fact. Thus we love and honor her as the Church personified and in doing so generate the perfection of Church in our own persons. Through her we learn how to accept Christ and His work and how to grasp the salvific, dynamic point of our ecclesial existence, viz., that true devotion to Christ is indubitably Marian in attitude.

Here for the moment, however, suffice it that we have simply lighted up the essential role of our missioner; for him to fall out of character is for him to be at any time unredeemed or unredemptive, to cease being Church-in-mission among men.

CHURCH: DIALOGUE WITH A DIFFERENCE

The "redeemed-redemptive" missioner, all other things being comparable, eminently qualifies for participation in dialogue on matters ecclesial. He can bring to it the dimension that makes the difference. His sensitivity for the pervasive and pivotal power of the Faith in our lives and his ability to witness Church, in a personal existence purely and simply saturated with the divine, are in great part the additives that put Christ in the midst of the two or three with whom he gathers together.

Now, may I refer briefly to a certain dialogue in the Church touching us as educators, refer just long enough to intimate at least some oblique illustrations of this difference, so worthy of our consideration.

Strategy in the Use of Manpower: As we discuss the "best" use of our manpower within the Church, talk travels off in two directions which eventually meet in what is insured against becoming a vicious circle no less by our spiritual depth and resourcefulness than by a sincere desire to serve and a practical common sense for doing so. In one direction we learn that strategy in deploying the troops will call for a priority list of needs in any given area of the vineyard, at home or abroad. We soon hear that in many ways we are in luck, for ours is the day of the sociologist, the economist, the psychologist, who just happen to be eager to lend a helping hand. We note, of course, that this is not just a list of needs being called for but a *priority* listing indicating what should be dealt with *first*. Next, in light of these priorities, there is to be made the choice of effective means, leading us finally to the projection of specific works. Excellent; but meanwhile the other safari has been on trail also. About at this point these discussants, coming in from the other direction, are beginning to come into sight—or earshot. They have been busy asking themselves: *Who* is this manpower in the Church, anyway? How broad, therefore, is the question of availability? How can we assess the talent and competence, the generosity discernible at the moment? And, above all, what can we learn and do about preparing and planning—effecting—a real (perhaps an explosive) deployment of Church everywhere? The primary grounds for hope, of course, are the folks doing the talking. If we ourselves are truly Church, great things lie ahead.

Light vs. Heat in Processes of Decision-making: In the practical order, strategic decisions that result in the choice of apostolic means in the Church, constantly in need as they are of more light, are precisely what the label indicates: involvements in strategy, which are often complicated for reasons beyond the imagining or accustomed range of either the statistician or the apostolic bloodhound. At the same time, the *donnée* of the decision-maker is always limited too, though he benefits from the grace of state and hopefully is closest to any significant detail that tends to complicate the situation.

The heat that is generated as we strive to join forces in dialogue for decision is often appalling. It nearly always takes a journalist, who is trying to keep bread on his table, to carry on for very long at all.

No one really needs to be told that more than schools and classes are involved in religious education, for the forming of truly committed Christians. No one actually denies that the ideal of religious formation is to reach all the members of the Church and to effect Christian community everywhere. No one with any degree of sensitivity experiences aught but joy in reading in that document from the Council that the sacred liturgy is the summit toward which all the activity of the Church is directed and at the same time is the font from which all Her power flows. But, then, perhaps those of us who hammer away forging the obvious do nevertheless tend to oversimplify matters on the practical level of implementing ideas. Our most recent expert* on the psychological topography of the changing world has discovered that those who favor change pure and simple for the ideal values they see in it are numer-

* Mary Perkins Ryan.

ically strong; but, she adds, they generally do not know solid ways to proceed. On the other hand, those who hold the reins of authority are generally thought to be long overdue in creating a more universal and healthy involvement of the many in the thankless task of leading us all. The canonical right to communicate with a superior directly is not enough.

More sophisticated, experimental structuring of these formal relationships within community is destined more and more to discover and develop talent on every level that will assist and eventually ease the way for the decision-maker. Obviously, such experimentation fosters formation in Christ and contributes to the making of Church. Should we say, "The administrator who is redeemed is redemptive" and hope that both processes might go forward together, as in life they must if they are to go at all? Better that the good things in these structured relationships arise from within as an outgrowth of positive sharing and experimentation by all of us who are in love with and motivated by the ideal, than that it be, as it were, *forced upon us* by increasingly embarrassing contrasts between our own procedures and the efficiency of the world around us.

The "Defense" of Catholic Education: That slender little book[2] caused quite a tempest. But what really were the issues? There are not enough schools? they are too costly? they are not producing? (The dialogue might be a dead giveaway here!) The author often claimed, of course, that she never really got a hearing

[2] Mary Perkins Ryan, *Are Parochial Schools the Answer?* (New York, Holt, 1964).

on what she considered the main issue, namely, the Church's manner of facing up to Her universal obligation and responsibility for the religious formation of *all* Her children, whatever their age or condition. The brilliant description of that responsibility, with its essential ties to the liturgy, must have registered with the blindest of her critics.

Meanwhile, a specialist is scarcely needed to spark a conversation on the burdens and weaknesses of Catholic school systems at home or abroad in this or any given existential moment. For instance, who can deny that Cambridge Overseas Examinations in sub-Sahara Africa tend to make minions of boredom out of Christian educators? That more than three-fifths of our Brazilian candidates for building up the Body of Christ cannot be made to wait on formal schooling? That conditions of segregation and social snobbery prevalent in some purportedly Catholic schools in Latin countries and elsewhere might impel the social scientist to recommend suppression and a regrouping of our forces? Or, that keeping abreast of the Joneses in the persons of the successors to the Manns and the Deweys, or remaining friendly with the agency accreditors and solvent with the financial creditors, is not always conducive to our projecting a redeemed and redemptive presence as educators?

But the times are too full for us to go on the defensive. As educators we face a simple truth: wherever we are laboring, the deepest human issues are involved; they lend practical range to our reason for existence in the work we are doing. We must face them squarely, constantly reappraise our approach, and remain imaginative and realistic. Meanwhile, whatever may be the instrumentality for producing (better, witnessing) Church—whether already existing or about to be brought into existence—it should be acknowledged for what it is and developed to the fullest, with due respect for circumstances. No apostolic endeavor owes an apology to another. Competition is wasteful only when it is sterile. And for even the most successful of us in the apostolate the parable of the barren fig tree, I am afraid, can be kept handy for an occasional meditation.

Theology for ANY Kind of Work in the Apostolate: The ink has flowed, as reported nationally, to get the reverend Sisters out where the action is, since the bulge in the Belgian book trade. The reassessment of our works, instead of the reassessment of our witness, has at times set the pendulum swinging mighty close to the jugular vein of our religious teachers—the Sister is sewing, the Brother is doing mechanical drawing, and the priest is almost anywhere. Some solved their embarrassment by hurrying through their teaching day, so that they might run off to work in the apostolate.

Really, the dialogue has taken some unpredictable turns, but in the long run it has thrown us all back on a restatement of an essential, supporting theology for the apostle at work wherever he is. After all, the missioner running the noodle machine simply has added complexity to the old rice-bowl routine and, for that matter, could not hold a Chinese lantern to the multimillions administered annually through the Church's participation in the help extended to the developing countries around the world. We have long known these efforts under the heading of pre-evangelization. Certainly there needs to be a quality about it to make it such. The teacher who ironically misses the apostolic rhythms of his classroom can scarcely be recruited for much more than a burst of athleticism outdoors. In these terms, it truly does not make any difference at all who is doing what—it will all be accomplished with about the same flat unredemptive results. And so the reverse should be true: with a real who at work, it will not much matter *what* he is doing. It will be redemptive. Now, again, what were those priorities?

Listen to the expert again. On the question of the theology of mission that strategically calls for the Church's all-out response to development work (education, health care, community development, social action): Eschatologically the Church is the *real* world, the perfected world. She is humanity full-grown in the resurrection. Christianity has eliminated the distinction between the religious sphere and the profane. Development work and evangelization must not be regarded as two entirely different activities—and if the profane world is built up by development and this world is to be redeemed and sanctified as well as possible by evangelization—as though the Christian were beside or above the reality of this world. Real development is Christianization. The central aim of the Church as a "sacrament for humanity" is to help complete humanity in its growth toward the Kingdom of God. Therefore, we are assured: *

* By Fr. François Houtart, of the Center for Socio-Religious Research in Brussels, Belgium.

1. "A priest or religious engaged in real development work really evangelizes and Christianizes.
2. "A layman, going in for real development, need not supplement and sanctify his task by doing explicit evangelistic work. His task as such is Christianizing.
3. "Development work is only Christianizing if it really humanizes.
4. "A clear grasp of the basic vocation of mankind and personal practice of virtue [being *Church*] are necessary to keep development work secure and effective and to make development workers develop into skilled operative [redemptive] forces.
5. "It is the task of priests and religious to live a most exemplary life in their work of development and in this way make God's fidelity and His creative presence visible in this historically pardoned humanity.
6. "Since the entire visible Church is called to cooperate in the completion of all mankind, the laity also must play an apostolic part in development work.
7. "There can be no conflict between humanization and evangelization."

Thus, again, the dialogue on our specific labors in the apostolate pivots really on our projecting Church; a redeemed presence in *any* work will ensure the redemptive quality that makes the difference. Material aid, without personal guidance toward the integration of the aid both mentally and morally, can spell chaos in social structures and even moral collapse in a people. The perfect example of development has always been the work of the educator who is striving to form the whole personality, not just dispense a little math or a few deportment cards.

TEACHING—NON SCHOLAE SED VITAE

All the goodness flowing forth so superabundantly from the Council, whether directly or indirectly, is experienced and appreciated in proportion to our own religious education and formation. All the challenge to change acts as a foil for our own Christian human excellence. All the conciliar winds that blow reveal our shapes and forms for what they are.

As a matter of fact, are we living and thriving through it all, and growing ever deeper in response to our holy religion? That means being spiritually invigorated, related to the world, moved toward Christian unity, and opened positively to all our fellow-men whoever they are.

If we are not, we are very likely not very good educators either. The apostolic spirit of our students would be a fair index. For the qualities we would be lacking are the very ones that we are called on as teachers to develop in them. Scripture says Christ began to *do and to teach.* Our most real task is to give fruitful witness. Example, as even the pagan knew, draws. *Church* is redemptive.

The student we are serving must experience the flowering of his precious and unique humanity through response, in grace, to the world around him. As we educate him, we might ask at regular intervals along the way:

Can he conduct his own affairs?

Does he know the answers, or the procedures for seeking them out?

Is his physical being understood and accepted by him?

Does he appreciate the range of his feelings and sensitivities?

Has he found God and embraced the habit of faith?

Does he know and love men and appreciate community?

Is he *open* enough to be saved; *humble* enough to be objective; *tough-minded* enough to live amidst life's complexities; *perceptive* enough to keep his bearings; *wise* enough to adapt for the best use of opportunity; *prudent* enough to handle the living moment; *religious* enough to allow room for mystery?

Does he come alive in Christ, experience the freedom of Christian existence?

Whatever the student's steady growth along these lines, if it is proceeding according to his grace and his natural capacities, thank God for our call, for we are instructing him unto justice.

The qualities of integration and relevance evident in all we do will find us habitually exercising him in faith, in freedom of choice, in self-knowledge, in holy hope, and in charity for God and neighbor.

Our love for him will be reflected in the language we learn and the land we adopt to serve him. We will not long be strangers to missiology or anthropology or psychology. No science of leadership formation or technique of group dynamics will pass us by. If English is being learned as a second language, that is the way it will be taught.

Missionary life will be kept vibrant by the exchange of ideas and the sharing of experiences. There will be pastoral solicitude for the great movements of the Church in liturgy, Holy Scripture, ecumenism, and the ecclesial mission. The role of the layman in building up the Body of Christ will unfold already in the young lives we see lived around us.

The Church shall be in mission.

The redeemed shall be redemptive—and the rose and the fire shall be one.

Collegiality and the Educator

REMBERT G. WEAKLAND, O.S.B.

> For it is the duty of all bishops to promote and to safeguard the unity of faith and the discipline common to the whole Church, to instruct the faithful to have love for the whole mystical body of Christ, especially for its poor and sorrowing members and for those who are suffering persecution for justice's sake (Matt. 1:10), and finally to promote every activity that is of interest to the whole Church, especially that the faith may take increase and the light of full truth appear to all men (*De Ecclesia,* No. 23).

This and similar texts in Chapter 3 of the Constitution on the Church show us how the individual bishop relates to the whole Church. Collegiality is simply a useful term to indicate that relationship in its fullness. We are tempted, I am afraid, to take this concept in too narrow a sense, to restrict it to legislative acts. It is true that the Constitution points out that "the power of binding and loosing, which was given to Peter (Matt. 16:19), was granted also to the college of Apostles, joined with their head (Matt. 18:18). This college, insofar as it is composed of many, expresses the variety and universality of the people of God, but insofar as it is assembled under one head, it expresses the unity of the flock of Christ" (*De Ecclesia*, No. 22). The theological foundations implied in these statements and the conclusions that come from the concept of collegiality are full of dimensions not yet totally probed within the Church.

From a theological point of view one can see more clearly in this concept how the Spirit works among us. The concept of the infallibility of the pope without the concept of the collegiality of the bishops presents too narrow a picture of how the Spirit of God is operating in the Mystical Body. We can now see the workings of the Spirit in its fullest theological dimensions. But again to see only the concepts of infallibility and collegiality without the concept of the people of God is also to miss a theological dimension in that working of the Spirit toward the fullness of Christ. These theological insights are not new to our age, but the further light thrown on them by the Constitution on the Church makes our age a unique one in its striving for Christian unity. Father Eugene Burke, C.S.P., has rightly pointed out that the truly pastoral character of the Church, founded on the collegiality of its bishops, is worked out in history as God's revelation in Christ becomes more deeply understood by our age—or any age for that matter—and is responded to.

INTERACTION NECESSARY

Collegiality involves sharing. We see it first of all as a sharing in policy-making, a sharing of teaching authority. But with this sharing goes also a sharing of responsibility. Our day has seen, in all phases of life, a need for all to participate in decision-making. This flows from the kind of involvement we are asking and from the maturing of our members. We find this in our civil and industrial corporations; we find the trend in religious orders; we find it in the Church as a whole. Because of the complexity of the civilization in which we live, I cannot say that this is a bad trend. On the other hand, it must also include the sharing of responsibility—a trait that requires humility as well as maturity. We can expect that in the Church as a whole more and more decision-making will be shared.

The pope has already taken steps to see that the collegiality of the Council continues in a synod of bishops which will act as a permanent body of counselors. By showing the individual bishop that his care and concern for his pastoral ministry cannot stop at the confines of his diocese but must extend to the whole Church, and by implementing this in a practical way, the Holy Father has made the role of the individual bishop take on a kind of universalism of responsibility that is serious and far-reaching. The bishop, in turn, must share his decision-making and responsibility with his clergy and people. So, in fact, must the religious superior.

We have come to expect that the pope, by reason of his position and office as head of the universal Church, has the vision to see beyond national boundaries and conflicts, beyond cultural traits and deficiencies, beyond the immediate and temporary, to a fuller reality of God's revelation to all. Now we are asking each bishop—and ultimately each Christian—not only to share that view but to be a part of the Church's universalism and the vitality of its cultural pluralism. Father Burke put it well when he said of the bishops as the successors of the Apostles that theirs was the responsibility "to evoke, stimulate, and sustain the apostolic mission of the Church." He further commented that "theirs is the responsibility for making each member of the Church aware of his mission responsibility for the whole of humanity called to God through Christ."

NECESSARY KNOWLEDGE

This shared responsibility will be meaningless—I might also say will be dangerous—if the knowledge that makes such a responsibility possible is not also shared. This means that each bishop must more fully understand God's revelation on one side and the actual world that is responding to it on the other side. What we are saying is that collegiality implies a broader and deeper education on the part of our bishops, and thus of our priests and people alike. It is not sufficient that the bishop know God's message, but he must also know the world to which it is being revealed today.

It is not for me to decide whether our bishops and our priests are capable at this moment of such responsibility and whether they have been educated to it. Our task regards more directly the future. It could, however, be safely asserted that many bishops when they first attended the Council were not aware of the breadth of the Church and its present status in those countries not classified under Western civilization. To many this awareness came rapidly and forcefully. It is difficult, nonetheless, to make up for lack of knowledge. Good will is not sufficient. Time and source materials are absolute necessities—commodities that a bishop finds it hard to come by. Deficiencies in our training are not easily remedied in later life. If this concept of the catholicity of the Church came to most of our bishops in a new light because of the Council, it cannot yet be said that it has reached the whole Church—all of us. This will require education and programs geared toward a fuller meaning of the Church and its catholicity.

CULTURE

The first burden, then, placed on education by the emphasis of the Constitution on collegiality is that of making the whole world, and especially non-Western cultures, known and understood and appreciated. The greatest merit of the Council to date has been the ability it has given us to see the Church as going beyond Western civilization. Until now, the Toynbees of our age saw the Church as dying with Western civilization. The Council has made it clear that such is not to be the case. Although the Church was decisively formative in the history of Western culture, Christianity, as such, is pancultural; it knows no such limitation. This does not mean that the Gospel message, when it comes in contact with a new culture, will not also become formative in that culture and perhaps even change it radically, but it does mean that we are able to distinguish in our Faith that which is the Gospel message from the national and cultural manifestations that it may legitimately have taken in the course of history. We are seeing more clearly today that whatever is good is Christian, wherever it may be found.

For these reasons the Council again spoke of a good pluralism within the manifestations of our Faith in different cultural ambients. The needs, physical as well as psychological, of every area of the world's surface are different, and so the emphasis will vary from place to place. This is not only to be expected; it is good. In the Constitution on the Liturgy it is emphasized that indigenous musical elements, for example, are to be used and preserved insofar as it is possible.

If collegiality, then, is to be a valid working principle within the Church, the needs of each locale and the cultural values and traits of non-Western cultures in particular must be known and appreciated—first by our bishops, but ultimately by all of us. Our present educational programs are based on Latin and Greek heritages that are slowly disappearing in favor of a mixed-scientific program. With all of this one cannot quarrel, but to it must be added a broader understanding of other cultures. In many school systems such courses have been added, but the difficulty of finding competent instructors is still an enormous one. For those who, unfortunately, are unable to receive such training in their high-school and college programs there is no solution but that it be obtained in the seminary. If our future bishops are to be properly informed, our future priests must perforce receive such education. It then must reach all of the people of God so that they may truly understand who is their neighbor.

To do this adequately we must go one step further in our educative processes. We have certain stereotyped concepts of other cultures that are arrived at by a kind of comparative basis. A certain exotic—sometimes even sinister—quality grows up in our minds about whole areas of the globe. Teaching geography, teaching history and politics are not enough to dispel these images and to implant a true notion of other areas. Even the sociological or economic approaches, although they tell us much about needs and stresses and tensions, are not complete enough. We must delve into the very thinking processes of a culture and its modes of expression. The meaning of that which just sounds exotic to our ear, or looks quaint to our eye, has to be probed for its meaning as communication. We are often stunned by the profundity we find beneath that which seemed so simple and picturesque at first glance. For this reason I would suggest that our missiology include not just political and economical approaches but the artistic as well. This level of teaching is most difficult on an international basis and the ground for it will have to be laid—and is being laid—by anthropologists, ethno-musicologists, and the like. Their results are reaching many of our missionaries, some of our bishops, and almost none of our people. This is the task of education.

TECHNOLOGY

It is also the task of education not only to show the missionary how modern technology can be used, but to show how that same technology can be used to educate the entire Church. First of all, that technology must be welcomed as a true gift of God. The concept of unity and of true collegiality would be impossible today without our communications system. We must say our *berakah* for it. We must use these same means to get to know the needy churches better, not just their needs, but who they are and what they are, and how they manifest the risen Christ within them. On all of these levels, both on the home front as well as in foreign missions, we have much to do.

The point that is most important here is that collegiality as defined in the Constitution on the Church makes all of this more imperative now than ever before. We have often complained here in the United States that many church laws and regulations seem to be made with Europe in view and are not apropos of our own situation. Are we to repeat now the same kind of mistake on a world basis? Are we not obliged now to look beyond our own dioceses, our own religious order, even our own pet missionary area, to a truly universal concept of the Church, that it may be Catholic? To do this we must educate ourselves first to a broader vision of all our human brothers. For, as Father Burke related, collegiality as the working of the Spirit within us involves all of us. It is "the supreme symbol of that brotherhood whereby, through Baptism, all Christians are brothers of the First-born of the Father."

Brothers Today in the Church of God

Luke M. Grande, F.S.C.

> It was the best of times, it was the worst of times, it was the age of wisdom, it was the age of foolishness, it was the epoch of belief, it was the epoch of incredulity, it was the season of Light, it was the season of Darkness, it was the spring of hope, it was the winter of despair, we had everything before us, we had nothing before us, we were all going direct to Heaven, we were all going direct the other way—in short, the period was so far like the present period, that some of its noisiest authorities insisted on its being received, for good or for evil, in the superlative degree of comparison only.

When Dickens penned these opening words for *A Tale of Two Cities,* he might as well have been speaking of the 1960's as of the 1770's. It is good to be alive in this "best of times"; it is bad to be alive in this "worst of times." It is an exhilarating, it is a depressing, era of flux in civilization, in the Church—or should we say reaffirmation. We are living with unrest; we are living with new hope. And in the midst of it all, definitive evaluation of what is going on is impossible. Yet we must attempt to assess our experience if we are to build upon it.

Despite the fact that historians tend to pigeonhole the past, as though it were simple and one-directional, people of every decade have gone through the unsettling soul-searching that we are going through today. So, although something new has happened in the past decade, it is good to remember that the insights and innovations of our Von Braun, Küng, and Schillebeeckx, though real and effective, will become a part of history, a part of a continuity. No matter how drastic today's scientific or theological "advancement" might *seem* to be—or *actually* be—it is a flowering; it has had roots, buds, blossoms, and will die to make possible further developing, budding, and blossoming.

Of the billions of years in the life of the cosmos, only the last 5,000 have witnessed the tentative beginnings of science with the creation of man; of that 5,000, the last 200 and of that 200, the last decade, curve to register a knowledge explosion unprecedented in man's history. Similar unfolding in the evolution of the spirit has exploded in new light and new excitement: Vatican II is history, but still exciting history; and the people of God will never be quite the same again, whatever the future might bring. "Xavier Rynne" may have let the cat out of the bag, but whether he had or not we would still be witnessing the renewal that we have today.

While Mars and the moon get closer and closer, and the accumulated knowledge of the physical universe becomes more and more staggering, the world of the spirit, of God and His creatures, takes on new dimensions; the crysaloid Church unfolds into ever more meaningful and beautiful forms.

Within this scheme fit new developments in philosophy, theology, the liturgy: these impinge in turn on the lives of the people of God; and, as a family of this people, the Brothers find repercussions not only in the superficial aspects of their daily lives but at times in their very fundamental conceptions of themselves. From macrocosm to microcosm, nature and man interlock in a unified but expanding world of matter and spirit. Situated in this world is the religious Brother and the nature of his apostolate is modified imperceptibly with the bombarding of myriad new relationships that occur in his world.

Philosophers, who have been known at times to hook "truth" unalterably to a given system that brooks no question or expects no refinements, are not nearly as complacent as they once were. Perhaps, after all, there is something new to be said by the existentialists or phenomenologists, a new world to explore.

Theology, it has been proved, need not be disguised philosophy nor an anatomizing of the bones of archeology, but is a revelation of the dynamics of God's plan in a time-eternity continuum: the history of salvation.

Morality need not be a legal description of a criminal code: sin—what kind, how many, with whom; was there grave matter, sufficient reflection, and full consent. Rather it can investigate how humanly man should act, why he acts as he *does,* and how he *should* act in order to fulfill God's law of love. (Such a direction might be damned wrongly for leading to "situational ethics," when in actuality it is merely recognizing the complexity of human acts.)

None of these areas (maybe they should be called arenas) is really sacred any more. Nor is the clerical scholar alone interested. Ideas, vital to the unfolding of the spiritual life of the people of God, are being picked apart by the Rosemary Lauers, the Daniel Callahans, *et al.*—the new and articulate laymen. Initials behind the name, whether representing academic titles or the writers' vocational connections, are not the criteria for credence; rather these criteria are the validity and maturity of thought involved in a statement.

Finally, re-evaluation of the religious life has become fair game in the general evolution. Like philosophy, theology, and morality, it must be taken in the context of the needs of our times which are, as Robert O. Johann, S.J., says, "to close the conceptual gap that exists between being human and being holy, between secularizing the world and sanctifying it, between man's creativity and his creaturehood." [1]

A first axiom is that the "spiritual life" is not ideally a kind of "angelism" (a conception sometimes implied in the word "spiritual") as it was at times conceived of in the past, a Jansenistic attempt to purify oneself from matter, from the world, with a purely negative asceticism that would effectively Platonize a man out of human existence. R. W. Gleason warns in his essay "That They May Be One" that to "by-pass humanity in order to reach God is an implicit denial of the Incarnation of

[1] Robert O. Johann, S.J., "Creativity Without Guilt," *America,* Vol. 113 (Aug. 14, 1965), p. 165.

the Son of God."[2] The religious life is a relationship between God and man; not between God and man's spirit, but between God and man with his intellect and will and emotions, a creature with hands and eyes and ears as well; he is a person with personal relationships; and the relationship between him and God radiates to other persons.

Paul J. Bernadicou, S.J., says: "If we come to understand the roles of *persons* in Christianity, we will be in a position to assess their role in the spirituality which underlies and motivates the religious life. For religious life is basically an intensified living of Christian human spirituality."[3] Religious are first human beings, Christians, then "religious"; and they are now reaffirming the fact that they belong to the human race. They are different from "humanists" because of their commitment: they have contracted to cooperate with God, through Christ, to "divinize" the world; they may not reject the world in order to contemplate, in Buddhist stoicism, their collective navels; they are social beings, hoping in a very real sense to bring heaven on earth. They are witnesses of Christ to mankind. And they all have this common role whether they are Jesuits or Franciscans or Marists or members of any of the other hundreds of religious families. Their ultimate goals, even their fundamental means, are the same.

From this starting point everything else follows: their religious vitality is assured in the social act of the liturgy. The Constitution on the Liturgy declares:

[2] R. W. Gleason, S.J., *To Live Is Christ* (New York, Sheed and Ward, 1961), p. 12.
[3] Paul J. Bernadicou, S.J., "Persons and the Religious Life," *Review for Religious*, Vol. 23 (Sept. 1964), p. 596.

> The liturgy is the summit toward which the action of the Church is directed; at the same time it is the source from which all Her power flows. For the aim and object of apostolic works is that all who are made sons of God by faith and Baptism should come together to praise God in the midst of His Church, to take part in the Sacrifice, and to eat the Lord's supper (No. 10).

Though each individual religious makes his own progress and develops into what God wants him to be at his own rate, he is part of a community in the process of "becoming" the people of God. The liturgical reforms recognize this human-spiritual need and have accommodated the action of the Mass to it. The "magic" character of worship (where effects are not caused or not commensurate with the cause) is eliminated by the community liturgy and the liturgy still retains the mystery of encounter between God and His people. Nourished in the course of the liturgical cycle, the religious with his intensified commitment through the vows and this reinforced social character through community, is prepared to enter into the apostolate in any of a multitude of forms.

SELF EXAMINATION

With a new sense of mission, religious are examining the value of long-established but unquestioned apostolates. The sanction of tradition does not necessarily vindicate their existence nor, on the other hand, are they to be rashly abandoned merely because they are long standing. But questioning and subsequent revalidation merely strengthens traditional apostolates and if they do not withstand scrutiny they are perhaps better scrapped.

Teaching orders, established by their founders to care for the poor, for example, are redefining the term "poor" and are wondering if the elaborate systems in which they have become involved are truest to the spirit of their religious dedication. As a result, isolated and monolithic congregations are learning to cooperate with other orders and are investigating new possibilities.

Students on secular campuses need religion as well as do those on the Catholic campus; and religious priests, Sisters, and Brothers are coming to the aid of the long-suffering Newman Clubs. On the levels of grammar school and high school the Confraternity of Christian Doctrine is booming, answering similar needs. There are even discussions concerning the advisability of Catholic orders selling their schools, and their members going into the public-school or college systems. Some orders already hire out some of their men to other religious congregations, and *Opus Dei* has for a considerable time operated within the framework of established nonsectarian organizations. The growing interest in the consortium between various colleges suggests possibilities for cooperation on all levels: with more or less success. Sisters' orders have ignored their differences, recognized their common ground, and worked cooperatively in grammar schools and high schools. Brothers, on the other hand, have been loathe to give up their autonomy—but how, if at all, are the goals or the means of attaining them of the Irish Christian Brothers, the Brothers of Mary, or the Christian Brothers different from one another? Is not the idea of a "distinctive" character largely a myth? Or, at least, not as potentially divisive as this has been allowed to become? Who knows, someday all three of these orders I have mentioned might be usefully consolidated into one. It is healthy, of course, to have states in a federal government, individual families in a social organization, and "family" orders in the Church structure, but there is nothing that indicates *per se* that cooperation might not be possible and good if the apostolate requires it.

Reform schools, diocesan schools, schools for the underprivileged, the disinherited, the handicapped, the mentally retarded—all are being dabbled with, in a spirit and movement which Bernard Häring describes in his article "The Catholic Church in Modern America": "The fixity of form due to sociological factors fell to pieces [within American Catholicity] to make way for a powerful synthesis between a true obedience to the demands of the Church's life and a courage to push forward to new fields." [4]

Catholic nursing orders might daringly invade city hospitals, take on work among the aged or mentally disordered—in cases where such orders have become identified with glorious, but expensive, mausoleums for the rich. Clinics for the poor, staffed by religious with M.D.'s, could well attract the idealistic and apostolically-minded young religious. Above all, the sense of

[4] Bernard Häring, C.SS.R., "The Catholic Church in Modern America," *The Catholic World,* Vol. 201 (April 1965), p. 28.

apostolate rather than of business must pervade community spirit.

LAY BROTHERS

Salvatorians, Jesuits, the Paulists have already deployed their forces in publishing. Television and radio offer other communications opportunities. But, perhaps, nowhere (among Brothers' orders, in particular) is there greater need for a radical sense of mission than among "lay Brothers"—those who do clerical or manual labor. In foreign countries—Africa, Pakistan, etc.—like Peace Corps workers, they will have a sense of mission, building chapels or roads or growing wheat and corn; but as other, only cheaper, hired hands, they are doomed to be unfulfilled unless imagination opens new and apostolic areas in which they can unfold as dedicated religious workers. It may be time to get them off the farm altogether and into something else. We cannot expect, nor should we desire, passive, lobotomized religious in any field, who would plod out their lives as though the *aggiornamento* had never existed. Nor should "blind obedience" or a vague stake in the apostolic labors of others be given to them as a justification for mechanical existence. Just how a sense of mission can be inculcated in the hewers of wood and drawers of water, I do not know; but it must be done.

Every man—and this includes the religious—needs a feeling of satisfaction, a sense of fulfillment, a realization that what he is doing is vital and worth while. His work must be his apostolate, his life; and, in a sense, his life must be his work. The Christian apostolate, of course, is not the same as philanthropic enterprise. W. J. Battersby says of De La Salle:

> He never pretended to be a philanthropist acting through love of his fellow-men. This is not to say that he did not have a very real affection for the poor boys in his schools. On the contrary, all his writings prove that he did. But this affection was inspired solely by supernatural motives: the salvation of souls and the spread of Christ's kingdom upon earth. The education of the masses, considered as an end in itself, was something he never envisaged. The slogan of the humanists of the nineteenth century: "we must educate our masters," would have had no meaning for him.[5]

In every type of religious labor the qualitative difference is essential; nevertheless, as the supernatural builds upon the natural, a religious who despises his work or himself can hardly look upon anything he does as an apostolate. His religious exercises must be integrated into this new functionalism: his schedule should suit the needs of the twentieth century, not those of the founders of the sixteenth, seventeenth, or eighteenth centuries; his reading, his meditation, his prayer life should be alive and affective, at his service sustaining him in his vocation. (The old adage that Sundays were made for man, not man for Sundays, has been lost in some orders.) Most of the fussing going on today in seminaries and houses of formation results from conflict between the forces holding with tradition

[5] W. J. Battersby, *Lasallian Meditations* (London, Waldegrave, 1964), p. 97.

and those crusading for adaptation. But that is a whole separate, though related, subject.

The implementing of a fresh approach to the religious vocation will be difficult and painful, but consciousness involves a risk not known to the anaesthetized. It is better to have fumbling attempts and brash error than ennui and complacency.

All religious orders are feeling the effect of the "new breed," of the young men in their novitiate and in their communities, but they are only one strain in the chorus of awakening and rewondering about man in the world today and are not to be feared. Rather they are to be thanked, for they give witness to the continued viability of the Christian message.

Religious orders are not dead; they are shaking themselves like bears coming out of hibernation. This can be a springlike period with opportunities for revivifying the ideal of the religious life and creating a fundamental sense of mission! The apostolate to "foreign" countries is meaningless unless it is merely one more facet of an all-embracing and less specialized mission to all men. It cannot be patronizing or statistical; basic respect for other races and their religious beliefs are essential to a "missionary"—whether he is in Selma or Johannesburg.

CONCLUSION

We must ransom the time. Newman wrote about a "Second Spring" (abortive, as it turned out); and we too are experiencing a "Second Spring" that is branching out of the Second Vatican Council. The possibilities for missionary renewal are great. It is perhaps too early to predict what the future will bring. If Brothers think with the mind of the Church, of John XXIII and Paul VI, they will remain alive and will be transformed into something perhaps different from what they now are, but something ever evolving and unfolding as favored families among the people of God.

Missionary Orientation of the Vows

M. Rose Eileen, C.S.C.

"Missionary" as well as "the missions" are terms which have been assigned new overtones in the contemporary world and which have taken on many new aspects as a result of the insights emanating from the discussions of the Council Fathers and statements in the Constitution on the Church.

We are in a state of renewal. As has been wisely remarked, Christian churches everywhere have the same needs for renewal—renewal in terms of sacramental life, of deeper penetration of God's Word in Sacred Scripture, of more dynamic personal response of the people of God to His Word in life and action—and all this to be effected in a secularistic, materialistic world and a world marked by an increasingly cosmic pattern of thought quite different from the world of only a decade ago. Yet, while "missionary" and "the missions" in their traditional implications are fast disappearing as the Good News of Christ is being communicated to the most remote peoples of the world, the concept of the "mission of the Church" in relation to every baptized person is coming to permeate more meaningfully and more deeply the thinking and action of the people of God. One has only to contemplate the statements of the Constitution on the Church to prove this point.

THE CHRISTIAN VOCATION

Every Christian, because he is a baptized person, is necessarily a missionary, and is engaged, or should be, in the universal mission of the Church. The Church, whether in Africa, Asia, Western Europe, Latin America, or the United States is a pilgrim Church and a missionary Church. Every member of the people of God, of the Mystical Body of Christ, is a missionary by vocation, if not by response; he is a missionary in virtue of his baptismal character and consecration.

Everywhere the Church is surrounded by a nonbelieving world; that world is not necessarily an unknowing world insofar as the Christian message is concerned. The fundamental tenets of Christianity are known, but not personally accepted in response. These truths inevitably must condition the concept of the missionary; whether he be a member of the laity, or a religious consecrated by vows, he must communicate the "Good News" to the world in which he lives.

Certain other principles in the traditional deposit of the Church's treasury of truth, but given new emphasis under the action of the Holy Spirit in our own day, must be invoked in this discussion if the essential meaning of our topic is to be carefully delineated. Granted that every baptized Christian is a missionary, the missionary apostolate is not to be regarded as an overflow, but as an integral part of the life of the Christian. But religious consecration through the profession of the vows as most clearly set forth in the sixth chapter of the Constitution on the Church is presented "as a sign which can and ought to attract all members of the Church to an effective and prompt fulfillment of the duties of their Christian vocation (*De Ecclesia*, No. 44). The Constitution further states, "Religious should carefully keep before their minds the fact that the Church presents Christ to believers and nonbelievers alike in a striking manner daily through them" (*De Ecclesia*, No. 46). Having set forth in the Constitution its chapter on religious, this important conciliar document treats the eschatological nature of the pilgrim Church and its union with the Church in heaven. The importance of seeing religious life in such a context is obvious. As an eminent theologian has remarked, commenting on religious in the context of the Constitution, "Religious life is a constant thrust toward the Parousia and a recapitulation of the Church of Pentecost." [1] Furthermore, the function of religious in the mind of the Church in this period of renewal is to collaborate with and animate the laity in the apostolic mission of the Church.

NATURE OF RELIGIOUS VOCATION

No relevant treatment of religious life and its professional consecration could fail to incorporate the principles stated above. Every aspect of the life of religious should be seen in an ecclesial focus. Perhaps

[1] Bernard I. Mullahy, C.S.C., Speech at the 1965 Superiors' Institute for the Sisters of the Holy Cross.

this statement has never had such deep significance as in the present life of the Mystical Body of Christ, the people of God, when its very nature, its function, its unique mission have been spelled out so clearly, so profoundly by the Council Fathers of Vatican II, acting under the charism of divine inspiration characteristic of a general council. Fundamentally, therefore, any consideration of the missionary orientation of the vows must begin by a statement of the nature and purpose of religious in the people of God as set forth in *De Ecclesia.*

The very order of development in that sublime document is not without significance. Before the important sixth chapter on religious, the preceding one in the Constitution is devoted to the universal call to holiness of all Christians. It is from this vantage point that the chapter on religious sets forth its principles:

> From the point of view of the divine and hierarchical structure of the Church, the religious state of life is not an intermediate state between the clerical and lay states. But, rather, the faithful of Christ are called by God from both these states of life so that they may enjoy this particular gift in the life of the Church and thus each in one's own way, may be of some advantage to the salvific mission of the Church (*De Ecclesia,* No. 43).

The Constitution continues:

> The faithful of Christ bind themselves to the three aforesaid counsels either by vows, or by other sacred bonds, which are like vows in their purpose. By such

> a bond, a person is totally dedicated to God, loved beyond all things. In this way, that person is ordained to the honor and service of God under a new and special title. Indeed through Baptism a person dies to sin and is consecrated to God. However, in order that he may be capable of deriving more abundant fruit from this baptismal grace, he intends, by the profession of the evangelical counsels in the Church, to free himself from those obstacles, which might draw him away from the fervor of charity and the perfection of divine worship. By his profession of the evangelical counsels, then, he is more intimately consecrated to divine worship. This consecration will be the more perfect, in as much as the indissoluble bond of the union of Christ and His bride, the Church, is represented by firm and more stable bonds.
>
> The evangelical counsels which lead to charity (*cf. Summa* II-II, q. 184, a. 3) join their followers to the Church and its mystery in a special way. Since this is so, the spiritual life of these people should then be devoted to the welfare of the whole Church. From this arises their duty of working to implant and strengthen the Kingdom of Christ in souls and to extend that Kingdom to every clime. This duty is to be undertaken to the extent of their capacities and in keeping with the proper type of their own vocation. This can be realized through prayer or active works of the apostolate. It is for this reason that the Church preserves and fosters the special character of her various religious institutes (*De Ecclesia,* No. 44).

It is then from the theology of the religious within the total context of the Church, the people of God, the pilgrim Church, the Church with a unique mission, that the missionary orientation of the vows must be considered. Perhaps it may be advisable to say at the outset, that while the juridic aspect of the vows has not decreased in importance, it is always more important that this juridic aspect be seen in the broader, deeper, and higher aspects of the theological foundations upon which the canonical and moral aspects of the vows ultimately rest. There is always danger that the focus may be distorted.

FUNCTION OF VOWS

The Christian life is initiated in Baptism when the baptized person becomes the recipient of the divine life of the Godhead and is constituted in the relation of adopted son of the Father, brother of Jesus Christ, and spouse of the Holy Spirit. From that moment until death, the baptized person is committed to the pursuit of holiness! "You therefore are to be perfect, even as your heavenly Father is perfect" (Matt. 5:48). What, then, is the function of the religious vows in relation to these relations and to the attainment of this goal? What is the function of each of the three vows in regard to deepening the reality of the relations with the Trinity and actualizing more effectively in daily life these relations in the pursuit of perfection like unto that of the heavenly Father? Are there not very important implications in this fundamental theological truth which should be spelled out, not only for the junior religious, but also for senior religious and for the youth entrusted to their care? Would emphasis on this reality perhaps be a means of eliciting attitudes of mind and responses of heart which might lead to a more serious consideration of religious life?

Religious profession is spoken of as "a second Baptism." Is this truth to be presented exclusively or predominantly from the negative point of view under the aspect of remission of sin and punishment? Rather religious profession should be presented as a second Baptism more especially and positively as a deliberate, voluntary, loving public profession that one is committed to pursue more perfectly, more fully, more wholeheartedly the relations established in the sacrament of Baptism through the vowed renunciation of all that would hinder the religious from the perpetual fulfillment of the conscious awareness and pursuit of the full implications of the relations of that religious with the Trinity of Persons in the Godhead. By the sacrament of Baptism the Christian is constituted a lay priest and witness to Christ in the people of God for the world at large. Through religious profession that function of lay priesthood and witness is not only more deeply radicated in the religious, but she is constituted a public witness of the holiness of the people of God. Again, *De Ecclesia* so beautifully says:

> Religious should carefully keep before their minds the fact that the Church presents Christ to believers and nonbelievers alike in a striking manner daily through them. The Church thus portrays Christ in contemplation on the mountain, in His proclamation of the kingdom of God to the multitudes, in His healing of the sick and maimed, in His work of converting sinners to a better life, in His solicitude for youth

and His goodness to all men, always obedient to the will of the Father who sent Him (No. 46).

The Church as the Bride of Christ lives the life of the risen Christ enthroned in glory while immersed in the pilgrim world here in travail and suffering. By Baptism the people of God, all members, have died to the flesh and been born into the life of the Spirit, even while living immersed in the things of space and time. For all the people of God, therefore, as the Constitution reiterates, there is a certain conflict between the yearnings of the supernatural life of the spirit and the actualization of their earthly sojourn toward the full and perfect participation in the beatitude of the life and joy and perfection of the risen Christ. But what is the relation of the vows to this conflict and tension between nature and grace which is the heritage of every member of the people of God on pilgrimage? Are the vows to be presented for the missionary, whether that term is used with restricted or universal connotations, as a complexity of laws of command or prohibition likely to stress tensions, rather than inspire positive, fruitful, joyous pursuit of holiness?

Perfection ultimately must have its source, its ideal, as well as its end in the Trinitarian life of the Godhead. But that Trinitarian life is essentially an infinite life of knowing and loving within the Godhead. A life of dedicated perfection must seek, therefore, the renunciation of everything that is an obstacle to the attainment of a more perfect participation in that life of knowledge and love. The end, therefore, is not a negative renunciation, but one that creates rather an emptiness like that of the chalice which at the words of consecration is to be filled with the Paschal Mystery.

POVERTY

Poverty must be seen not merely as limiting the use of material goods to prevent jealousy and discord, or to effect a superficial equality, or to accumulate material goods for the increase of resources for the apostolate in which the religious or his community is engaged; but rather as a challenge to an ever deeper spirit of detachment from all that might not only hinder, but fail to contribute positively to an ever deeper unifying love binding together all the people of God, whether religious or lay, and uniting all in the bonds of an ever deeper personal union of love with Christ.

Religious poverty, ultimately, is not a renunciation, but an exchange! The exchange of possession of temporal riches of this world for spiritual riches! "Blessed are the poor in spirit"—detached, dependent—"for theirs is the kingdom of heaven." Daily, as missioners, the people of God pray, "Thy kingdom come!" But it will come and the religious will further its coming, whether in the strictly so-called mission lands, or anywhere in the world where souls are to be brought to the love of Christ, only if their spirit of detachment is lifted up as a sign of the Church, as a sign of the holy pilgrim on journey to beatitude. The missionary aspect or orientation of the vow of poverty will be emphasized, not by a series of "don't's" and "do not have's," but only when that poverty is seen as an indispensable means of conforming the religious to the poverty of Christ and to the independence of the Godhead from all material things which, nevertheless, have their origin and causality in Him and Him alone! The religious, while dependent on some material goods because of her psychosomatic nature, nevertheless by her vow of poverty, is freed from undue concern, so that she may participate more fully in the divine joy of God's inner life, in order that she may communicate more perfectly and fully the spiritual treasures of this knowledge and love to the people of God in the fulfillment of her role in the mission of the Church. A proper balance between the negative and positive implications of the vow must be effectively communicated to religious, if they are to be formed in the apostolic missionary spirit, whether at home or abroad. Their idea of renunciation must not merely embrace detachment from a particular room or material object. Their poverty must be the more difficult total detachment of spirit from one's own cultural patterns of life and thought in order to adopt and adapt to those of an alien people; it must be the renunciation, not infrequently, of the easy mode of communication through one's native tongue for the somewhat hesitant, faltering, inadequate flow of the language of those to whom we minister; it must be the renunciation of the familiar sights and sounds of one's own social milieu for, perhaps, the strident, irritating context of another way of living! Their poverty must be of this deeper order if they are to be true witnesses to the poor Christ and bring the Word of God to those to whom they are sent in the name of the Church. The spirit of detachment must give testimony both to service and to actual poverty, a duality of function and of implementation not easily understood or effected, but certainly worthy of serious thought and effort.

OBEDIENCE

Religious obedience reflects the very life and unity of the Trinity. In obeying perfectly, supernaturally, devotedly, and consciously the will of legitimate authority, there is manifested in the religious family a union of wills like unto the oneness of the divine will in the Trinity of Persons and unity of nature. But the religious must be brought to realize the relation of the will of the superior to the will of her first superior, the Supreme Pontiff, and to the will of the heavenly Father from whom all authority is derived.

The religious in fulfilling the perfection of the vow of obedience must come to see that by so doing she participates in the very act of submission wherein Christ was obedient unto death, and thus more deeply radicates and perfects the participation in the priesthood of Christ with which she was endowed in the sacraments of Baptism and Confirmation, thereby becoming in a special way a victim with the eternal Victim. Her every act performed according to the virtue of obedience thereby comes to be an act of worship to be offered together with the supreme worship given the eternal Father by the divine Victim for the salvation of the world!

CHASTITY

The vow of chastity in its missionary orientation, as from a more general point of view, must be rooted in love and a love that is a fruitful love. The religious must be formed in the science and art of channeling natural maternal instincts rooted in her womanly nature, to the supernatural level of attracting others to the fullness of divine love and thereby fulfilling their missionary vocation! "As Father Durwell writes: 'Christian virgins have taken up their abode at the heart of the Christian mystery of redemption.' Their souls are an altar on which Christ is immolated each day for the redemption of His Body which is the Church; their very being is a source of intensification of life for the Church. In giving their body to no one, they give their soul to everyone" [2] and through their apostolic service, no matter what it may be, they are disposing others to receive and increase divine life and to be formed in Christ. The bridal relationship established through Baptism is radicated and actualized more fully by the religious profession whereby the religious is identified most intimately with His Mystical Body in its mission to bring the divine Trinitarian life of love to all men. Martyrdom is the supreme mode of witnessing to Christ. Red martyrdom sacrifices the preservation of the individual; but the preservation of the species as such which is sacrificed by the vow of chastity constitutes the religious as a white martyr whereby she is, in the

[2] William F. Hogan, C.S.C., *No Race Apart: Religious Life in the Mystical Body* (Stonehill College, Mass., 1965), p. 42.

language of one theologian, "related to service, to fellowship, and to witness in a special way to the 'otherness' of God." The vow of chastity is designed to make of the religious a contemplative in action, thereby giving to others in love the perfect goods of the spirit. What is this but fulfilling the mission of the Church to which one is consecrated at Baptism? If the vow of chastity does not make the religious freer to give the good things of the spirit to others, it is not effective. As St. Thomas says in his treatment of virginity:

> It is necessary to the multitude not only that it should be multiplied bodily, but also that it should progress spiritually. And hence the multitude will be provided for sufficiently, if some give themselves to the work of carnal generation, and others, abstaining therefrom, give themselves to the contemplation of divine things.[3]

And this, for the glory and well-being of the people of God.

Not only on the day of profession, the day of their final acceptance as religious by the Church, but in the day by day pursuit of the perfection of their vocation, religious must come to see the profession of their vows and the fulfillment of them in the context of the total redemptive mission of the Church. They are always and ever the consecrated daughters of the Church, thinking with the mind of the Church, which is the mind of Christ, and acting in a union of love with the Church in every circumstance, living to the hilt through

[3] *Summa Theologica* II-II, q. 184, a.3.

their vowed dedication the perfection of their baptismal consecration.

As missionaries, their confrontation in this period of history will be largely with the great non-Christian religions and ideologies of the world—Islamic, Hebraic, Hinduistic—or one of the multiple paganistic forms of worship; or more frequently, perhaps, with that ideology of the total negation of religious belief which is atheism, more than a confrontation with unenlightened, semi-civilized impoverished peoples in some remote region of the world. Everywhere these ideologies are and have been making an impact on the thinking and mode of action even in the most Christianized areas of the world! Ultimately, the mission of the Church is to dispose these people to respond to the Paschal Mystery in all its fullness! These teeming millions and their respective cultures are still waiting for the convincing sign of the holiness of the people of God epitomized in religious—"the sign lifted up among the nations"—the Pentecostal sign, authentic, dynamic, transforming, pointing ever to the transcendent reality of a God who loves His people with the infinite love of the redemptive Incarnation and is loved here and now in this present existential order in total consecrated response of love, a love that can give all rejoicing. It does give all: ownership of materialities and all that poverty of spirit implies; it makes a joyous renunciation of the freedom of men for the submission which gives the glorious freedom of the vowed children of God; it makes the exchange of purely human love for the transfused love of consecrated virginity. And this total gift is made with urgent longing to participate more effectively in the redemptive mission of Christ prolonged in space and time through His Church, thereby giving to men something of a revelation of the love of the Triune God operative and made visible here and now, that men in turn may respond in love to that divine love!

The New Dimensions in the Apostolate of the Religious Woman

BERNARD COOKE, S.J.

There seems to be no doubt but that we are witnessing a very profound reassessment of the religious life at the present time. While some of this is due to the fact that the entire life of the Church is undergoing examination and reorientation and many new influences have come into the life of religious men and women, it is also due to the fact that we have never thoroughly thought through the specific reality of an apostolic community. To some extent the development of religious life in the Western Church has been a gradual adaptation of the original monastic structures, and most attempts to radically rethink and reconstruct religious life have met with more than limited opposition. Hence the question of the nature of the apostolate of the religious woman is one that we must raise very seriously, and attempt to give at least some tentative suggestions of an answer. To introduce some order into my remarks I will deal first with the religious as she works in activities of her community, then with her involvement in activity beyond the corporate works of the community.

APOSTOLATE WITHIN THE COMMUNITY

One of the things which should be stressed when one speaks of the role of the religious woman within her community is that in this situation she works in the life of the Church, not as a hired hand but as a member of an apostolic community. No one, of course, would subscribe formally to the fact that she is merely a hired hand; yet I think that in altogether too many cases the practical situation puts her rather effectively in that role.

If one accepts the fact that she is working as a member of a community, then it means that she is truly, in a personal way, sharing in the entire apostolic vision of her particular community. In order to do this she must have a clear understanding of the precise operative objectives of the smaller religious house in which she finds herself in a given appointment. Only if she does have this sort of understanding of the overall purpose of her community is she really sharing in that which is most basic in the formation of any given human society. Human beings group into genuine communities insofar as they genuinely share a common purpose.

If one does not share personally, in his understanding and decision, this purpose of the community, it is hard to see how he is functioning fully as a member of the community.

Second, we must remember that the religious woman engaged in apostolate does not lose her identity as a Christian. As a matter of fact, she has gone into religious life in order to dedicate herself more exclusively and more formally to the apostolic life of the Church. In our own day I think that this type of motivation is becoming more prominent in young people who come into religious life, and I think that in some cases we have lost some of the most promising young candidates for the religious life precisely because they have not found the opportunity to retain within the novitiate a clear consciousness of being apostolic Christians.

If the religious woman is a Christian, she must have some knowledge of the role her community plays in the life and apostolate of the Church. This is not just a question of giving her that understanding of life which is necessary for her human fulfillment. This knowledge is necessary also for the development of her life of faith. Faith is meant to be an intelligent participation in the faith-life of the Christian community. Faith is meant to be a life lived in understood fulfillment of the baptismal commitment by which one became a member of the Church. Certainly the religious, having joined an apostolic community in order to lead the kind of intelligent existence which is her right and responsibility, must have some understanding of where her community fits, of its position in relation to the life and goals of the whole Church.

This touches, of course, the question which religious, young and old, are asking today. The fact that we may have difficulty answering these questions should not keep us from discussing them openly with all the members of a religious community, allowing them also to contribute their understanding as to what our purpose might be. It is clear that in some instances this openness to all the members of the community, to their questions about the role of a given religious community, can be an anguishing affair. It may force a community to reassess the apostolic works that it has undertaken, to see if they are the ones most effective and most appropriate at the present moment of the Church's life. But if such questioning is taking place, perhaps we should regard it as part of the working of the Spirit in our midst. It is the Spirit who is responsible for the religious vocations of the people who have come to a given community.

Again, because she is a Christian, the religious woman is obligated to a life of prudence and decision. Since decisiveness lies at the very heart of the life of grace, it is impossible for a religious—or anyone else in the Christian community—to attain to mature sanctity unless she becomes a decisive person. She must acquire the capacity to commit her own Christian freedom to a definite course of action. Now obviously, if a person is to develop such prudence and decisiveness, one must have the opportunity to exert in freedom a certain amount of initiative. This opportunity to exert initiative in no way militates against the genuine meaning of authority and obedience within a religious community. Genuine authority is meant to direct, to guide, such initiative, in some cases even to originate it and to stimulate it. Genuine obedience is to direct but never to replace that spirit of freedom and exercise of initiative which every human being, including the religious woman, requires if he or she is to attain to genuine maturity as a person and as a Christian.

APOSTOLATE OUTSIDE THE COMMUNITY

There is a second large area which our question today raises, an area which is somewhat new: the apostolic activity of the religious woman beyond the assigned task which she has in her community. In this regard a preliminary remark must be made, a remark which may be somewhat startling but which we must examine carefully and with honesty. Despite the fact that the religious vows are a very basic and far-reaching commitment of a person's Christian life, the corporate life of the religious community does not totally absorb the Christian or human existence of the religious involved. One sometimes has heard in the past that in coming into religious life the man or woman religious gives up all other rights, exists only for the life of this particular religious community. This cannot be, for one still remains a Christian with the rights and obligations that that entails, one remains a citizen of a certain country with the social obligations and rights accompanying that, one remains a human being with the fundamental orientations of the basic nature which we share. None of these can, in the last analysis, be ceded. One must be careful that one does not, by extending the demands on time and energy that a religious community can legitimately make, deprive the religious woman of the means of fulfilling her responsibility in other areas.

I realize that this is a very delicate issue, one for which no hard and fast rules can be given. It is something which has to be worked out in the pragmatic give-and-take of everyday existence. But it is one which must be worked out with honest appreciation on the part of religious superiors that they are not the total masters and lords of the life of those who are in their community.

RELIGIOUS AS PROFESSIONAL PERSONS

This problem becomes more pressing today because we have an increasing level of professional competence among religious women. The acquisition of competence in intellectual spheres or in social techniques, whatever it happens to be, bears with it its own responsibility and its own rights. When one becomes, for example, a member of the intellectual community, one cannot remain indifferent to the intrinsic demands of that community.

Again, while there must be careful evaluation of the respective responsibilities of the individual religious woman, the religious community cannot ignore some of the legitimate demands upon this person which the Church or human society can make at the present time. There are certain needs which the Church has, certain needs of human society, which perhaps critically demand the attention of a given religious because of his or her talent or professional training. And the religious community must face the responsibility of freeing this person to undertake a task which lies outside the corporate activity of the community. As a matter of fact, it might well be that one of the most apostolic efforts some religious communities can make at the present time is to prepare some of their members for almost total involvement in vital apostolic functions which are not part of the ordinary assigned apostolic activity of those communities.

One of the points that should be mentioned in this regard is the need and the obligation of religious communities to cooperate, particularly in the sharing of highly talented personnel, for the sake of the Church or the advancement of mankind. There are many tasks in the Church at the present time which demand the close cooperation and team effort of very high-level, technically-trained persons. In many cases it is impossible to find such a team within a single religious community; and the Church's life and the betterment of mankind can only be advanced if these people from various religious communities have the opportunity and the freedom to work together to attain something which none of them could possibly do as an isolated individual. It is perfectly clear that this means a great sacrifice on the part of a given religious community which has planned on utilizing a person in its own corporate apostolate, and which in preparation for such work has spent several years and a considerable amount of money to prepare the person. Yet, the greater good of the Church should be seen as taking precedence in such cases, and the given religious community may well be bound by charity in this regard.

Today we are asking many questions about the purpose of religious life and the value of our own apostolic contribution to the Church. People are writing books on who the nun is and what she should be doing. Perhaps the only point on which all agree is that no one for the moment has ultimate answers. It is difficult to foresee the precise apostolic needs of the immediate and more distant future, difficult to orientate our religious communities toward the right type of apostolate. In this difficult situation of choice and policy-making, religious communities must remain open, must listen carefully to the needs of the Church and the needs of mankind. Concomitantly they must listen carefully to the apostolic interests of younger religious. All this may well indicate the will of God which we must crystallize by our decision.

What the role of the Sister will be in the years ahead we do not know, but this much seems clear: It can no longer be a simple unquestioning participation in a task undertaken decades ago and never seriously reassessed. The day has passed when a religious is to be simply a warm body filling a job whose value is questionable. Let us hope that it has passed forever.

The World's Work in the Day's Work

JOHN J. CONSIDINE, M.M.

The story goes that someone reminded a Red leader in one of the Latin American countries that the Bolshevik party in Russia had less than 40,000 members in 1917 when it took control of the Russian people numbering 182 million.

"That's not so remarkable," the Red responded. "With 100 cells of ten persons each, properly trained and dedicated, I could take over this whole country of ours with its five million inhabitants."

In the United States at the present moment there are some 14,000 residences of religious Sisters, most of these residences with 10 to 50 Sisters assigned to them. To me, 14,000 residences constitute cells of influence for impregnating the Catholic population in the United States with commanding ideals—for instance, with fiery zeal for the world apostolate.

VISION FOR THE FUTURE

The work of North American priests and Sisters in Latin America in turn produces finer ideals among

Catholics in the homeland. Bishop Primeau of Manchester, named by the Bishops' Committee for Latin America as Episcopal Coordinator for U.S. personnel in Latin America, points out the advantages that can accrue to the Church within our borders.

"I end," he declared in a recent statement, "by reminding all who bear the responsibility for the United States contribution to Latin America that they will not only give; they will receive. I feel that we North Americans are going to garner from our work in Latin America much knowledge of new work and new structures, new answers to the social revolution that is not to be confined within the borders of Latin America but is already permeating the entire world. Latin America can give us new enthusiasm and new vision. It may well be that we in North America will find in Latin America the true answer to our racial problem, to our problems of reunion, our ecumenical problems."

The spiritual vitality and vision pervading the 14,000 residences of women religious in the United States will most certainly be influenced by the experiences of our United States church in Latin America. But conversely as well, Latin America and the entire missionary world will be influenced by this very same factor of spiritual vitality and vision found in the mass of Sisters' convents throughout the United States. It is a two-way street.

This breadth and depth of vision must reach all of us early in life. I feel sure that the major superiors of women will agree that the great commanding ideals of religious life are ordinarily not acquired after one's election to a top post in one's community. They come in the early and intermediate years of one's career. These ideas and ideals take their practical form as Sisters assume their first responsibilities in the various convents of their community included in these 14,000 residences to which we have made reference.

Thus the rank-and file Sister of today is the mother provincial, the mother general of tomorrow, providing the inspiration, the guidance, the pace of accomplishment for hundreds, sometimes for thousands, for whom she is responsible, according to the insights which she acquired as a junior member of her community.

Hence it is obvious that to be truly efficacious the world's work of the Church must figure in the day's work, and in the day's work not merely of the mother general or the mother provincial. It must likewise be the abiding consideration of all, down to the youngest individual member of the community.

I recall as an innocent young priest on a visit to a bishop in India years ago asking the bishop if he made it a practice to talk over the problems of the Church in India with the missioners under his charge.

"Look, Father," he replied with a sternness which at the time I did not understand, "I expect my missioners to get up at daybreak and to work steadily until dusk and into the night on the job to which they are assigned. As to the problems of the Church in India, Father, I'll take care of those."

It is safe to say that there will always be some major superiors who will live under the fear that if their subjects take their noses off the grindstone of the day's work, the day's work will not be done. However, most of us now recognize that in this age, when all of us regardless of circumstances must rub elbows with the whole human race, it is essential to the day's work that each and every one of us keep our eyes focused on our obligations as members of an ecumenical Church.

Is it not, then, more than merely academic for superiors everywhere to reflect on the Red leader in Latin America who acts on the assumption that he can capture an entire nation if he properly guides 100 cells of ten persons each? Is it not quite practical to believe that a mother general who properly guides her convents of well-oriented Sisters can similarly influence the ideals of great numbers of human beings in far-reaching achievement?

WORLD OUTLOOK

What are the touchstones of the spirit that inspire a community of Sisters to vivid sensitivity to "the concern for every neighbor" which Pope Benedict XV declared to be the Christian ideal?

The half dozen conceptual ingredients which, I would say, should characterize the ecumenical outlook of every convent of religious are the following:

Ingredient number one: the breadth of Christian love. Pope Pius XII in the encyclical *Mystici Corporis* informs us that our first requirement for world outlook is this specific quality of the virtue of love. "First of all," stated His Holiness, "let us imitate the breadth of His love. . . . The love of the Divine Spouse is so vast that it embraces in His Spouse [the Church], the whole human race without exception." [1]

Ingredient number two: disinterested love. Again it is Pius XII who advises us. Man's failure in serving others, he notes, comes in great part from his insisting on doing for them what he selfishly regards as best rather than what objective, selfless wisdom would determine to be best. "To dissipate the misunderstandings, to prevent the conflicts or to calm them, we see only one sound solution," declares His Holiness, "namely, that of Christian charity, heroic, universal and disinterested."

Therefore, serve Latin America, Asia, Africa, all mankind, with disinterested love, wisely seeking informed and authorized leadership.

Ingredient number three: an abiding consciousness of the presence about us of all men, and of our obligation to exercise concern for all men. As Catholics we possess an immense treasure, our developed moral sense regarding our individual obligations of a personal order. But this of itself can represent narrow selfishness. We must understand our collective obligations. We must possess an abiding consciousness of people, of multitudes of people, not only of our neighborhood; not only of our city, not only of our nation, but of many peoples, of continents full of people, of all mankind. And we must have a keen sensitivity to the human condition of our fellow men on every continent. Without this, Christianity is a travesty.

Ingredient number four: a clear appreciation of

[1] Pius XII, "The Mystical Body of Christ," America Press edition, No. 113.

the Christian concept of the individual. Do we properly prize man as such? Man's excellence flows from genuine values:

1. Every man possesses a being given him by God and the power to enter into prayerful dialogue with God.
2. Every man possesses moral unity with all other men, equality, dignity, nobility.
3. Through grace every man can elevate himself to an intimate life with God.
4. Every man has a basic right to the material world to serve as his aid in purposeful living.

Ingredient number five: an appreciation of the Christian teaching on society. Society is not a mere aggregate of men. Christian philosophy describes society as a supra-individual unity to which every person belongs—there are no outcasts. There is active and passive sharing by individuals in that mutual supplementing one of another which brings out their potentialities, integrates their individual selves, calls upon their responsibilities.

The ideal religious is unfailingly conscious of these responsibilities to human society, which may be represented by five concentric circles, each a symbol of a successively larger social body: (1) the family; (2) the community; (3) the social or cultural region; (4) the nation; (5) the world, embracing as it does the entire human race.

Ingredient number six: Sixth and last of what we label as the touchstones of the spirit which will inspire us to continuing concern for our neighbor of the human race is a recognition of the great commanding Christian social concepts which represent liberty, equality, and fullness of life for all men on the globe. These are:

1. The right of every individual to civil and religious freedom.
2. The right of every individual to an education.
3. The right of every individual to the protection of his health and to engage medical facilities.
4. The right of every individual to preventive, protective, and remedial measures against poverty and destitution.

So much for these half dozen "ingredients" which may serve to maintain the abiding world outlook which already exists in so many of the local convents of our religious communities of women.

The great St. Augustine centuries ago evoked for us a marvelous vision of world society.

"The heavenly city, while it sojourns on earth," he declared, "calls its citizens out of all nations, and gathers together a society of pilgrims of all languages, not scrupling about diversities in the manners, laws and institutions . . . but recognizing that however varying these are, they all tend to one and the same end of earthly peace."

For true achievement for God in her service of man, every Sister recognizes that she must build on more than mere dutifulness to God.

Every convent of Sisters must possess within itself a vivid interest in, respect for, and regard for man.

Each such group of Sisters, then, must translate

this interest, respect, and regard into terms that will capture the fascination of every schoolboy. Thus will each convent constitute a cell for impregnating the Catholic population with its world mission.

Collegiality, Mission, and Laity

THOMAS E. CLARKE, S.J.

The purpose of this chapter is to provide material, focus, and some stimulus, for discussion on the topic: "Collegiality, Mission, and Laity." Hence I am not putting forward any theses, though undoubtedly I will reveal certain personal inclinations and even prejudices. The direct thrust of my remarks is theoretical rather than practical, and what follows will help to bring the presentation into closer contact with the concrete actualities which are the primary concern of many.

Let me order these remarks under five somewhat discrete headings, and then conclude with a summary and a few questions.

FOUR ESSENTIAL POINTS

First: It is of great importance to root pastoral concern in sound doctrine and vital theology, and conversely, to keep theological reflection in constant touch with the actualities of pastoral experience, problems, and needs.

Second: It is important to see that, for the Christian, the contemporary thirst for the unity of all mankind has its roots in God's great plan of salvation, whose goal is precisely unity, reconciliation, peace; the unity of man with man, of all men with Christ and through Christ with God, and of the entire creation through man and Christ with God. The goal is unity—that all may be one, that all may be summed up and restored in Christ.

Third: Collegiality is not a purely juridical reality, but is a sign as well as reality. Collegiality is sacramental, revelatory of that deeper fraternal communion which unites all the bishops and all the churches. I would suggest that, to avoid the pitfall of looking on collegiality as a purely juridical or administrative aspect of the Church's life, we speak of the mystery of collegiality, and relate it to the central Christian mystery, which is a mystery of unity in distinction.

Fourth: I would propose that we reflect on the need of thinking of collegiality (and of mission and laity) in the context of our own times. Father Burke has developed two important aspects of the world of today: socialization and nationalism. I would place special stress here on what is perhaps a more basic fact of contemporary life: secularization, secularity. I do so not only because it is a central concern at the moment, but because it has special pertinence to the role of the layman in the Church's mission today.

COLLEGIALITY: UNITY IN DISTINCTION

The first general point I would like to discuss is *collegiality* as a mystery of unity in distinction. In its narrow sense, collegiality has to do with the distinctive mode in which the supreme authority of teaching and ruling is exercised in the Church, by all the bishops of the world together, with and under the bishop of Rome. The theological problem raised by collegiality is the problem, we may say, of the hierarchical one-and-many: If the Bishop of Rome is supreme, how can all the bishops together be supreme? Either he is just another bishop, with a tiara instead of a mitre, or they are really just his delegates to the local churches, whom he sometimes will consult in important matters. Now the Constitution on the Church of Vatican II enunciated the fact of collegiality, but it did not propose a theological explanation. A good number of theologians have done so, both before and since. I personally find appealing the explanation according to which the Bishop of Rome never really exercises supreme authority alone. Even when he does not formally consult the rest of the episcopacy, he cannot govern the universal Church except as head of the *collegium,* as the voice of all the bishops, as a kind of corporate personality in whom they are mysteriously present and acting.

If we accept this view of collegiality, then perhaps we may better see how it is a mystery, a mystery of unity in distinction, and therefore part of the central Christian mystery which, at the most basic level, is precisely a mystery of unity in distinction. The supreme instance of this mystery we find within God Himself, where Father, Son, and Spirit are one, yet distinct. "Philip, he who sees me sees the Father." "I and the Father are one." Though this Trinitarian mystery—which the Fathers called *perichoresis* or circumінcession, that is, mutual indwelling—far transcends the mystery of collegiality, it should dispose the Christian to understand collegiality a little better.

In the person of Jesus Christ, the God-man, the second basic instance of unity in distinction is verified. Here, too, the Fathers of the Church spoke of *perichoresis*, circumincession, mutual indwelling. The one Christ is both God and man: divinity is not dissolved in humanity, nor is humanity absorbed by divinity. Yet he who is God and he who is man are one and the same *he*. Mary's Son and God's Son are one and the same. Again the mystery of unity in distinction.

At the third most basic level, the relationship between Christ and His Church, we encounter the mystery again. "Saul, Saul, why are you persecuting *me*?" asked the risen Lord. "*We* were buried together with him by baptism unto death . . .", Paul later wrote. The mystery of our unity with Christ while remaining our distinct selves: When *He* died and rose, somehow *we* died and rose. And conversely: *our* sufferings are somehow *His* sufferings. It is not we who live, it is Christ who lives in us. We find in Him ourselves, and Him in one another, particularly in those whom He has appointed to teach and rule us: "He who hears you hears me."

This mystery of unity in distinction could be studied in its many other ramifications. What concerns us here is its collegial form within the hierarchical Church. It has quite rightly been suggested that collegiality describes not only the relationships of bishops among themselves but the mystery of Christian brotherhood, communion, and community at every level, what I would somewhat ponderously call ecclesial *perichoresis* or circumincession or mutual indwelling. If we take collegiality thus broadly as the ecclesial dimension of the basic Christian mystery of unity in distinction, then we find it everywhere within the universal and local Church. Each bishop in his diocese represents all the bishops, and he represents the Bishop of Rome. Each local church stands for the universal Church and makes it present and visible in this geographical area. The parish priest is the presence of the bishop to this particular parish. The entire parish, clergy and laity, especially in its Eucharistic celebration, is an incarnation of the entire diocese and indeed of the universal Church in this neighborhood. We could go on and on. It is easy to note the obvious and important presence of the entire Church and of all the local churches to each of the needy churches. In the course of the following pages, I will be treating of three further instances of ecclesial *perichoresis:* (1) the presence of the ecclesial in the secular; (2) the presence of the Church and Her hierarchy in the laity; (3) the presence of the Christian churches to one another.

SECULARIZATION AND SECULARITY

My second point concerns secularization and secularity as the primary challenge to the Church and Her mission in our times. The Constitution on the Church in the Modern World leaves us with the task of working out, both theoretically and practically, a style of Christian thought and living which, not by way of mere pragmatic accommodation, but by way of deeper insight into the mystery of the Church and the world, will enable the Church to fulfill Her saving mission in our time. It is obviously impossible to develop here a theory of Christian secularity. Let me confine myself to a few remarks which will, I hope, be clarifying. And first, an effort at description (rather than definition) of terms:

1. By *secularization* I mean the process by which, over a period of many centuries, and indeed throughout the history of Christianity, with increasing acceleration in recent times, values and institutions of a political, economic, cultural, and, in brief, this-worldly nature have been disengaged from the direct and hegemonic control of institutional religion and Christianity.

2. By *secularity* I mean the attitude of mind and style of life which look upon the process of secularization with favor and sympathy, for whatever reasons.

3. By *Christian secularity* I mean the attitude of mind and style of life of the Christian who finds in secularization not only no threat to the Gospel, but a legitimate and even necessary explicitation of the Gospel regarding the relationship of the Church and the world, the Kingdom of God and the city of man.

4. By *secularism* I mean the attitude of mind and style of life which consider God, Christ, religion as irrelevant for man's this-worldly concerns.

I would further note that, from a theological point of view, there may be room for speaking also of the *mystery* of Christian secularity as yet another aspect of the Christian mystery of unity in distinction. The order of secular values, of the temporal, is given in Christian secularity a sphere of its own, relatively autonomous and distinct from the sphere of the sacred, the spiritual, the churchly (in the institutional sense). And yet Christian secularity is far removed from secularism. For the latter, religion and Christianity are simply irrelevant for the development of the values of the city of man, the values of this world. For Christian secularity the whole of human life and the whole of creation have been profoundly touched by the Incarnation of the Son of God, so that nothing human, nothing created, can be unaffected by the Christian mystery. It is in this sense that I have suggested that ecclesial *perichoresis* is applicable to the presence of the ecclesial in the secular. At the moment theologians may have a very imperfect conception of how the distinction of the secular and the sacred is compatible with the unity of creation and redemption, but Christian faith must perseveringly affirm the fact of this compatibility and act on this affirmation. Perhaps it is only when Christian secularity has been lived for a significant period that its theological justification may be more adequately elaborated.

THE CHRISTIAN LAYMAN

This discussion of Christian secularity brings me to the third general point which I would like to make; it concerns the Christian layman, his status and role in the Church and in Her mission. The emergence of Christian secularity and the emergence of the Christian layman are co-efficients. For the layman is, by definition, the Christian in the world, working out his Christian vocation, giving his Christian witness, in and through his dedication to the secular city. Here too our basic notion of unity in distinction, of ecclesial and apostolic *perichoresis*, is applicable. Where the layman is, there the Church is. Where the layman is, there the bishops are. The apostolate of the laity is the Church's apostolate, which means the apostolate of all of us insofar as, all together, we are the people of God.

The key distinction here has been made for some time by a number of theologians, and now has been authoritatively endorsed by the Constitution on the Church of Vatican II (what follows is largely citation or paraphrase of Chapter 4). Namely: there are two senses of the term "lay apostolate." There is first of all that lay apostolate which is incumbent upon every layman by the fact of his Baptism and Confirmation, which is a participation in the saving mission of the Church, which has as its goal to make the Church present and operative in those places and circumstances where only through the laity can it become the salt of the earth. This is an apostolate conducted in and through the secular, in the ordinary circumstances of family and social life, from which the very web of their existence is woven. In this apostolate the laity work for the sanctification of the world from within as a leaven. They make Christ known especially by the testimony of a life resplendent in faith, hope, and charity. This apostolate, which is the primary apostolate of the layman as such, and of all laymen, is contrasted by the Constitution with an apostolate to which *some* laymen are called, and which consists in a more direct cooperation in the apostolate, not precisely of the Church, but of the hierarchy.

I will not elaborate on this key distinction. But it is of primary importance for such practical problems as the relationship between the Christian layman's participation in the work of secular overseas organizations and his participation in the work of Church overseas organizations.

ECUMENICAL COLLEGIALITY

The final aspect of our theme on which I would like to touch is the ecumenical one. And here I will be relatively brief. On the level of theological principle I would suggest that in the relationship between the churches we may have an instance of the mystery of collegiality (in the broad sense of fraternal communion) which may be of primary importance for the task of helping the needy churches of the world. I speak from the viewpoint of a Roman Catholic, for whom the mystery of God's communion with mankind and of men among themselves in Christ has its primary visible expression, its sacrament, in the Roman Catholic Church. But, as a Roman Catholic, I also believe that the mystery itself is verified and even manifested outside the confines of the Roman Catholic Church. More particularly, in some, at least, of the activities of the other Christian Churches, I find not only the presence of God and Christ but the presence of the Roman Catholic Church, so that we may now speak not only of an ecclesial but of an ecumenical *perichoresis* and collegiality in the broad sense. Every time a Protestant minister baptizes, it is the one Church which is baptizing, which is present, and all of us baptized are somehow present. There may be room for a similar application of the idea of ecumenical collegiality in every Christian proclamation of the Word of God. According to Father Avery Dulles it may be said from a Roman Catholic standpoint that the Protestant Churches exercise a true prophetic function, and do so in intimate relationship with and dependence on the prophetic office entrusted to the Roman Catholic Church. There might well be important implications, even in the practical order, of such a conclusion. It seems to me that the sincere and open Roman Catholic will look upon the Protestant missionary ministry with mingled joy and sorrow: he will be sorrowful because, in his conviction of the truth of the Catholic faith, the fullness of grace and the Word is not being communicated by this ministry; but he will also rejoice, because grace and the Word are being communicated and, generally, in a notable degree. What is more pertinent to our theme of ecumenical collegiality, he will rejoice that somehow, in the mysterious design of God, that God who is able to raise up children of Abraham from stones, that God who does not need our human schemes and techniques, the one Church of Christ, which he believes to subsist in the Roman Catholic Church, is present and acting in the missionary ministry of the other Christian Churches. This is what I understand by ecumenical collegiality.

SUMMARY

Let me conclude with a brief summary and a few questions. We have been speaking of several realities, Christian and human, ecclesial and secular, upon whose confrontation and integration, theoretical and practical, the work of the Church today depends. We have spoken of *collegiality*, not only in the strict and technical sense of the relationship of the bishops in their governing of the universal Church, but more broadly as the ecclesial and ecumenical dimension of that fraternity and communion, that unity in distinction, which is the essence of Christianity. We have spoken of *secularity* as the central force of our times, with which the Church must reckon in her work of evangelization. We have spoken of the Christian *laity* and its mission under the double aspect of participation within the secular in the mission of the Church, and cooperation within the spiritual in the mission of the hierarchy. We have spoken finally of *ecumenicity*, and introduced the question of whether and how we may conceive of an ecumenical collegiality among all Christians. And all of this: collegiality, secularity, laity, ecumenicity, we have spoken of in the context of mission. Most of what I have said concerns the interrelationship of these several elements of our theme: collegiality, secularity, the laity, ecumenicity, the mission to the needy churches. For example: *secularity and the laity:* Should we allow and even foster a shift of emphasis in the mind of the apostolic laity from specifically Christian organizations to secular ones? *Secu-*

larity, laity, and mission: What about the Peace Corps and PAVLA? Is it to be *either* the Peace Corps *or* PAVLA? Is the layman more of an apostle in one than in the other? Is there some way, not only theoretically but practically, of viewing the relationship as one of complexity? *Collegiality and laity:* What are the respective roles to be assigned to clergy, religious, and laity in the total work of evangelization of an area, and what is to be the participation of the laity in the formation and implementation of basic evangelization policy? *Laity and ecumenicity:* Is there more room for a common apostolate of Christian laymen from different Churches within the secular apostolate of the laity than within the spiritual? *Collegiality and ecumenicity:* When, if ever, should one Church, with limited missionary resources, consider that the mission of another Church to one of the needy areas of the world is presently a sufficient representation of the Christian witness in that area?

Finally, I would only propose as an appropriate symbol of all that I have said, with the prayer that it may preside over the future, the words of our Lord which have been so central to ecumenism, and which suggest something of the profound mystery of collegiality as Christian communion and brotherhood: "Father . . . I pray for those who . . . are to believe in me, that all may be one, even as thou, Father, in me, and I in thee; that they also may be one in us, that the world may believe that thou hast sent me."

A Protestant Perspective

Gerhard Elston

I do not write primarily as a separated brother because I often do not feel separated. I speak to you as a layman who looks at the lay apostolate from personal experience. I speak as a historian rather than a theologian. I represent a kind of semi-ecclesiastical role because those of us who, for one reason or another, end up as full-time employees of either the Church or one of its subsidiary organizations have a very difficult time maintaining the integrity of our laity, or our layness. I place a slightly different perspective on the very concept of the word laity and speak of laymen, thinking also of the *De Ecclesia* definition, simply as the people of God. We laymen concede that the clergy are occasionally included. I wonder whether the distinction between the clergy and laity, between the religious and the secular, is really as valid, even within the Church, and within the people of God as we have been led to believe.

We on the Protestant side of the ecumenical movement learned to appreciate some time ago that there are quite profound theological differences between us, but these differences do not necessarily run along confessional lines. There are new lines being drawn in the world today which make, and are increasingly making, traditional distinctions anachronistic. Some of us believe that the whole vocabulary and the stance of the cold war has been made totally anachronistic by technological developments. I sometimes think that the theological divisions and the ecclesiastical divisions under which we all suffer have become outdated.

Frankly, I am not a missionary. I do not envy any Protestant or Roman Catholic missionary who has the task of explaining to a committed Hindu, Buddhist, or Marxist (particularly if he is academically trained or has majored in philosophy or theology), the real, actual distinctions between the various Christian professions. This is a task that I am sure many of them are called upon to undertake continuously. I doubt whether any of them cherish it. In many situations it is not possible to make such an explanation reasonable.

I speak as a Protestant and as a layman, but I do not speak for either laity or Protestantism. There is no one who can. There are tremendous divergencies in Protestantism. I speak from the perspective of the traditional churches. Even within these we have had a continuous experience of this division that does not run along confessional lines. Many of the things that I hold with considerable commitment will not be held valid by quite a few of my colleagues perhaps, and certainly not by a great many of my elders and betters in the church.

THE CHURCH

The first thing that needs to be noted is that we Protestants have a very profound conviction of the existence of the Church in the world. This divides me from a great many sects in Protestantism that have a completely different definition of what the Church is. I have essentially an historical, traditional definition of the Church expressed simply perhaps as the Body of Christ, of which we are all members. I believe very firmly that the Church is not divided, that it cannot be divided. There are true distinctions between the visible Church and the invisible Church that theologians make. Yet it seems to me that with full awareness of all the differences and distinctions that exist, when I say the Church I do mean the totality of the Church. I have much less difficulty seeing the Roman Catholic Church within that totality than I do for instance with some of our fundamental brethren. It is a great agony for some of us to try to determine how they also somehow belong in the totality of the Body of Christ.

I grew up in Nazi Germany. Somehow for me the essence of the Church is not predicated upon structures or buildings but on the survival of the Christian presence, the Christian witness, the Christian community. Those who still see themselves within the framework of a church under persecution know why they want to be considered part of a body that witnesses. When it becomes uncomfortable and dangerous one does not retain this sort of concept. The kind of crisis that erupted in Europe, whether you take the Nazi period or the more extreme periods of persecution under various forms of Communism in Eastern Europe as a basis, places the Church all over the world in one body. Compromises and distinctions are not easy to locate. The Church as an institution and a structure is ill prepared to face up to crisis, simply because it has too much invested in institutions.

UNITY

There is an essential unity to mankind. We see this at least in part in creation and we see it in the total redemptive work of God. The intention of the Creator certainly is for all men to be united in Christ. In a sense this was already accomplished on Calvary. A Christian who sees salvation for himself in this act of sacrifice on the Cross and sees the definition of love in this sacrifice cannot help but know that it was not for him alone. In every other person, you meet the person for whom the Lord gave His life.

We are forced to understand that He is Lord in the Christian perspective, and in the Hindu and Buddhist perspectives as well. We must become sensitive to what our Lord is doing in these other communities. This opens up a question of the wider ecumenism. Those of us who work with foreign students have to face this at all stages. This is both exciting and difficult because it raises questions of the historical continuity and of the essentials of the Christian faith and the structure of the Church. The true test for the Church is its ecumenism, not its structure or hierarchy. If the pope is supreme are the bishops simply his delegates to local churches or, in a sense, are the bishops not so much delegates to local churches but rather delegates from local churches?

Rather than see the Church in its hierarchical structure I would like to see the Church in the laity, as the Vatican II documents do. This turns a lot of things upside down and gives some exciting possibilities. Perhaps we can be helped by seeing the laity as the whole people of God, as the community of which the head is the Lord in the biblical image. Frankly the role of the Bishop of Rome is something that we Protestants are really going to be very happy to leave to Catholics to decide. It concerns us very profoundly, because we feel ourselves much involved. We have not had the willingness to admit that we are in fact separated. We do believe very strongly in the unity of the Church. Collegiality describes not only the relationship of bishops among themselves, but the whole mystery of Christian brotherhood and communion. Each bishop in his diocese does not represent the Bishop of Rome so much as the Bishop of Rome through the other bishops represents the Christian community.

I knew few institutions that are as secular as religious institutions frequently are. This is neither good nor bad but a fact of life. Of course, it depends to some extent on how we define secularism or secularity. Christian secularity, and of course this is the crux, pertains to the Christian who finds in secularization not only no threat to the Gospel but a legitimate and even necessary extension of the Gospel regarding the relationship of the Church and the world. The notion of secularism is the attitude of mind and style of life which consider God, Christ, and religion as irrelevant to man's worldly concerns. Nowhere else do I find the attitude on secularism as difficult to handle as when it appears in the Church. Many committed Christians (and I am speaking here of Protestantism) really do not see why some of us are so passionately concerned as Christians with Vietnam, with Latin America, with any place where injustice is being done, where babies die of starvation. To me this is a Christian concern precisely because the whole Faith is very relevant for man's worldly concern.

PRESENCE

We have gone through a series of changes of jargon. First we spoke of evangelization, then it was mission, then we preferred to talk about witness; the present "in-word" seems to be presence. I would say presence and participation. They all say the same thing. As to what Christian presence in the world means we have recently defined ecumenism as the churches talking to each other, being in relation to each other, together doing their task in the world. When can a church doing work in the mission field accept the work of another church as adequate and sufficient? The answer at its very simplest is at the very moment when we recognize in each other the Church, fully, completely. Both of us have to learn really what it means to be one body and that no human insufficiency can really separate what the Lord had created. He is calling us to a task which requires distinctions that are very important but not crucial to the life and witness of the Christian community. In the living out of our ecumenical commitments, in the mission (in Africa, or the New York suburbs, or the Chicago slums) we will find not only unity but a proper perspective on theology.

If you take this secularism seriously, why is it important whether the Peace Corps or a Catholic mission program is the relevant place to witness the vocation of the layman? The worker-priest movement in France raised this question and it is a question that has not been answered yet by Protestants or Catholics. Why cannot the priest work through secular agencies as well as religious ones?

From the Protestant perspective, of course, we are stumped by this beautiful phrase, "the priesthood of all believers." It justifies almost anything we laity want to do. But it always puts this into a priestly function. If one has a totally sacramental view of life and sees actions in life as a priestly function, it still is not very helpful if he does not live so well. This is precisely why people like myself who, after many years in various kinds of work for the Church, have a terrible time defending the fact that we are indeed professionals but still laymen nevertheless. When we go to a college campus, for example, the lay status is something to be cherished, for it gives entry to theological conversations. Nobody wants to argue theology with somebody whose professional duty it is to be a theologian. People are often puzzled by those who have other professions but take theology seriously.

PAROCHIAL STRUCTURE

It is not just the laity who must learn to understand vocation. In terms of what is happening we must change rather radically some of our present concepts of a vocation to work. We in the laity must understand our vocation differently. The mere fact of the establishment of a Church created such a huge range of problems that we no longer know how to live unestablished. I am not talking primarily now about the fact that there is a hierarchial structure that just grew up within the Roman Empire and that therefore we talk about the Roman Catholic Church even when we include Byzantine Catholicism. The whole parish idea of the Church is built on the Roman urban organization. Protestantism in America happens to be rural and has never really known what to do with the parish structure when it goes back where it came from: the city. The trouble with the original urban organization, not only in the Roman Empire, but right through the Middle Ages and the periods of the wars in Europe, is that it is defensive. Build a core in the center and a wall around it. It sent people out with special missions but there was no concept of the Christian community as a missionary community.

The World Council of Churches made a study of the missionary structure of the congregation. This amuses me. The congregation by definition almost definitely does not have a missionary structure. It has an essentially defensive structure. We do find a Christian community in other places here and there, on the campus, in the factory, in the Army, in the Peace Corps. But it is very hard to establish it in terms of anything that is more than simply present. Financially, of course, the Church is highly dependent on its parish structure. These other things are regarded as a sort of authentic and experimental manifestation of Christian community, but they do not usually raise money; they only absorb it. When the structures are removed forcibly then the Church usually has not had difficulty in finding its role and the role of the laity in the community.

These are some Protestant thoughts on the lay apostolate, Protestant but pertinent. We pray that the future will see a melding of Protestant and Catholic thought and apostolates.

The Mission of Government Service

PHILIP H. DESMARAIS

The achievement of spiritual purposes or religious objectives through service in the government is a provocative and delicate issue.

In *De Ecclesia*, Chapter 4, on the laity, we read: "The laity, by their very vocation, seek the kingdom of God by engaging in temporal affairs and by ordering them according to the plan of God" (No. 31). Some sincerely suspicious people or cynical types might interpret this charge as a directive for a policy of penetration of temporal organizations by agents of the Church in order to turn them into instruments of religion.

APOSTOLATE IN GOVERNMENT

Personally, I have no such fears. There is a rapidly growing body of opinion that one can exemplify the highest levels of Christian charity, in these times, through government service in programs on both the national and international levels. In service to children through education, in the war on poverty, in the struggle to eliminate racial injustice, and in the never-ending effort for peace in the world, there are unparalleled opportunities to work for these goals by serving in the various government programs.

How often have I heard from my colleagues in the government this point of view: "I believe I can do much more to aid my fellow men and to work for the most urgent priorities in charity and justice for all people through my job in government than I could in any religious organization that I know of at the present time."

This may sound like an unduly harsh judgment on the current activities of organizations of the Church, but I would rather view it as a reaction to the practical realities of the three-pronged crisis of poverty, race, and peace. Moreover, these realities confront not only ourselves, but all mankind today.

In our own country, we have made a national commitment to tackle the paradox of poverty at a time of unprecedented prosperity in the United States. This is, indeed, a work of the Lord and the Lord will consider as given or refused to Himself the charity given or refused to the needy. "As long as you did it for one of these, the least of my brethren, you did it for me" (Matt. 25:40).

In his economic report to the Congress last January (1965), President Johnson stated this paradox and indicated that it can and should be overcome.

> Americans today enjoy the highest standard of living in the history of mankind. But for nearly a fifth of our fellow citizens, this is a hollow achievement. They often live without hope, below minimum standards of decency.

> The per capita money income of these 35 million men, women, and children was only $590 in 1962—against $1,900 per capita for the Nation as a whole.
>
> We cannot and need not wait for the gradual growth of the economy to lift this forgotten fifth of our Nation above the poverty line. We know what must be done and this Nation of abundance can surely afford to do it.

The challenge abroad is even more stark and sweeping. To put it bluntly, according to a recent report by Barbara Ward, it is almost without exception the Christian—or, should one say, post-Christian?—societies that are exceedingly rich while nearly everyone else is exceedingly poor. Owing to the fantastic growth in Western wealth since the war and perhaps especially since 1960, the gap between rich and poor is widening further. Between nations with a per-capita income of between $1,000 or $2,800—largely around the North Atlantic—and two-thirds of humanity with per-capita incomes of less than $100, the abyss in amenities, opportunity, comfort, food, and health is as great as the biblical gap between Dives and Lazarus. We know what happened to them.

SOCIAL INVOLVEMENT

The response to these challenges by Christian men and women has been somewhat of a paradox. On the one hand we find the religious becoming more prominent participants in various fields of social action. American nuns are throwing themselves into civil rights and anti-poverty struggles. "When nuns join picket lines to protest the denial of human rights," says Sister Bertrand Meyers of the Daughters of Charity, "they are merely responding in new ways to the traditional question of how we can best bear witness to Christ." One of the prominent religious has doffed her veil in order to take a top-level assignment with the Job Corps. Priests, rabbis, and ministers are on the picket lines. Nuns, priests, and Brothers are in the forefront of the struggle for the improvement of public schools in Chicago. The outstanding Agency for International Development project in Peru is a credit union organized by a Maryknoll priest. The Office of Economic Opportunity has assigned major responsibility for the anti-poverty program in the State of Mississippi to the Catholic Diocese of Natchez-Jackson. The diocese will undertake a seven-million-dollar program in basic education and job training for the disadvantaged youth and unemployed adults.

While all this is going on, the hierarchy in this country and particularly in Latin America is recruiting as many laymen as they can get, to work in the educational and religious apostolate of the Church. Laymen became increasingly active in the commissions of the Vatican Council. The final session of the Council saw many bishops utilizing laymen as expert advisors for themselves and their participation in the discussions and debate. These developments are very exciting and in some ways very confusing to many people who are accustomed to the more traditional role of the laity and the clergy in the eternal effort to carry the principles of the Gospel to all mankind and into every sphere of human life.

POVERTY

Here in the United States the Economic Opportunity Act of 1964 is the coordinating spearhead of the new war on poverty.

What does the Economic Opportunity Act provide? The *Job Corps* is designed to serve the needs of hundreds of thousands of rural and urban young Americans who are out of school and out of work or who are employed in dead-end jobs. These youth, age 16 to 21, are eligible to enroll in the corps, which offers a rewarding opportunity for education, vocational training, useful work, recreation, and physical training. They will live either in conservation or training centers in rural or urban areas. These centers will be residential and will accommodate approximately 100 to 200 youth in the rural areas and larger numbers in the urban Job Corps centers.

There are nonresidential *work-training programs* for unemployed young men and *women,* age 16 through 21. These programs, to be conducted in the metropolitan areas, give particular attention to work opportunities which will enable young people to maintain regular high-school attendance. These programs are sponsored by state or local public agencies and by private nonprofit organizations. Work opportunities can be developed in hospitals, playgrounds, local government departments such as recreation, health, sanitation, public works, schools, settlement houses, and other places where public service can be performed. The Federal Government will initially make available 90 per cent of the cost of developing these work projects.

There is also a provision for a *work-study program* for needy college students. Colleges receive grants to pay for student employment on campus, as well as for off-campus jobs, in various health, welfare, recreation, education, and social service areas—especially where there is a pressing community need for the assistance of capable college students in programs which are part of a community's efforts to combat poverty.

The Economic Opportunity Act also authorizes the urban and rural *Community Action Program.* An integral part of the Community Action Program is the support and development of services for children in low-income families, such as preschool training, day-care programs, special health services, remedial reading and other noncurricula education programs, to provide the extra help that these young people in poor neighborhoods need if they are to keep up with regular school programs.

Participation by the widest possible range of community organizations is envisaged, provided, of course, that the programs they offer are available without discrimination throughout the community. Settlement houses, citizens associations, YWCA's and YMCA's, Protestant, Catholic, Jewish, and other youth groups, and similar organizations would all have a role to play.

Several hundred thousand of our fellow Americans have enlisted in the anti-poverty war. This past summer, some eighty thousand volunteers participated in the Head Start program for preschool children.

In a professional or technical capacity, thousands more are working for the Job Corps, the Neighborhood Youth Corps, and in the VISTA volunteer program.

With the enactment of the Higher Education Bill, we will begin enlistment of both new and experienced teachers into the National Teachers Corps. These people will be assigned in teams to teach in the most difficult settings in urban slums and isolated rural communities.

The reputation of the Peace Corps is already legendary. Now in its third full year of operation, it has provided an opportunity for 25,000 dedicated Americans, mostly youths, to serve in dozens of countries while living with the poor and helping them to help themselves in improving their own lot through projects in education, agriculture, community development, road building, and improvement of health and living conditions. The Peace Corpsmen somehow have been able to avoid being linked with "missionaries." The policy of the Peace Corps has been the same as the admonition of the Franciscan Bishop of Boga, Indonesia, Most Reverend P. N. Geisc. "In a poor country," he insists, "we who come with the message of salvation must live poorly, build poor buildings, and take on the poverty of the place. When people complain, 'Your school won't last ten years,' the Bishop replies: 'But it fits the environment, doesn't it?' "

OPPORTUNITIES EXPANDING

The opportunities for service to one's fellow-men in the poverty program and in the Peace Corps are gaining an ever-widening response from the youth of America. This is a tribute to the generosity and dedication of our young people. It is proof that they are willing to forego the materialism and affluence of this most affluent society in the history of mankind and give totally of themselves. These developments leave some questions unanswered, however. Can the ultimate oblation in Christian charity be provided through government service? Can a total moral commitment be made within the limitations of government action? Governments are not notably equipped to undertake moral judgments or objectives outside the dictates of national law. National policy enmeshes itself in a tangle of motives when it becomes a major instrument of moral considerations regarding people of other nations—as evaluated and defined by politicians and bureaucrats. Mixing policy and morality can lead to righteousness, exaggerated expectations, the offending of sensibilities, moral recriminations, and emotional reactions needlessly complicated by legitimate political considerations.

"What specifically characterizes the laity is their secular nature," states *De Ecclesia.*

However, the new Constitution on the Church goes on to chart this course for the apostolate of the laity:

> Therefore, by their competence in secular training and by their activity, elevated from within by the grace of Christ, let them vigorously contribute their effort, so that created goods may be perfected by human labor, technical skill, and civic culture for the benefit of all men according to the design of the Creator and the light of His Word. . . .
>
> Moreover, let the laity also by their combined efforts remedy the customs and conditions of the world, if they are an inducement to sin, so that they all may be

conformed to the norms of justice and may favor the practice of virtue rather than hinder it (*De Ecclesia*, No. 36).

The call is clear. Government service is only one answer, but a powerful and pertinent answer. It deserves an attentive hearing.

Lay Structure for Lay Responsibility

THOMAS QUIGLEY

Our topic in some ways presents a false issue yet demands a decision. We agree on the propriety, the rightness, and the absolutely essential role of the layman's involvement in secular structures, specifically in governmental structures. The role of the layman is to be effective, to be wholly Christian, to be in areas where real things are being done. He has to be in touch with and in some way affecting the vital structures of today. Society has developed in such a way through the course of the centuries that today the government plays an increasingly important role. One need not justify or attempt to justify Christian participation in government but rather should seek to exercise more effectively his apostolate, his Christianity, through government service. Let us address ourselves to some correlative problems.

PROPER PLACEMENT

A problem for the ardent apostle is to find the proper lay structure in which to serve. There is no listing or pool of job opportunities within the United States Government. It is difficult to wade through government publications and discover an opportunity for talented people to exercise their apostolate. Many people who have doctorates would like to work in the government field but there is no one person who can act as a liaison for these competent and interested lay apostles. Those interested in achieving Christian goals through government work must search continually to locate the best, most effective position. Yet the information gap is not quite as complete as some may feel. The responsibility to inform the 195 million people in this country of the kinds of opportunities available lies not with governmental agencies, even though they all have recruitment programs.

In our context we are primarily concerned with speaking to the 45 million Catholics in this country. How can we inform them of their obligations? We can profit by what has been done along the lines of the lay apostolate within Christian communions outside the Catholic Church. Some church groups have provided information listings and different kinds of information for people who are interested in serving overseas as Christians but not within Church structures. For example, the overseas personnel section of the Committee on American Laymen Overseas of the National Council of Churches in New York has published a listing of sources for employment overseas in a brief booklet of basic information. There is a need within the structures of the Catholic Church to provide similar literature.

Other publications of the Committee on American Laymen Overseas include *Can Your Faith Travel,* with suggestions for American laymen who will be working overseas but not as Church-sponsored personnel. The greater contact and cooperation between individual Protestant personnel directors and their counterparts in the Catholic Church will bridge some of the communication gap between the Catholic and extra-Catholic communities.

We must caution against an excessive detailing of the lay apostolate. In recent years we have had a healthy reaction against requiring lay apostles to be involved with Catholic action under the direction of the hierarchy. There is a wider dimension of the lay apostolate, that of just being a Christian. However, if our laymen, our dedicated people, feel that they must in all cases be in a secular structure then we will suffer. For example, the White Fathers were looking for a sociologist to go to East Africa to help with sociological research in order to renew and evolve pastoral structures and pastoral approach. If a dedicated person who could do this task felt that he must not work in close association with the ecclesiastical structure, the Church will suffer. The determining factor should not be whether a person is under the direction of the hierarchy with a mandate but rather where he can best accomplish something as a Christian and show forth the presence of Christ in the world today through his fellow man. A person ought not be prejudiced in favor of nonecclesiastical forms. We can recognize that the ecclesiastical institution is a part of the world, not something out there with the world somewhere else. It is one of the structures and we can easily work within it if we feel it is relevant and significant. One can make a contribution within the Church as well as outside of it.

The individual must make his own decision about where and in what kind of institution, Church-related or not, he can serve the world best. Essentially he is not to be an assistant in evangelization but a layman fully exercising his Christianity in and to the world.

LAY MISSIONARY VOCATION

A very splendid talk by Father Coleman Barry, president of St. John's University in Collegeville, Minnesota, had as its theme that Catholic educators have a weighty responsibility to promote the idea of service to the community and to their fellow men in their regular educational programs. He pointed out various approaches to this concept which should be presented. He mentioned the traditional Catholic vocational idea of becoming a missionary. Often the only thing a student in a Catholic school hears about international service is from missionaries who speak at the school recruiting future members for the order or religious community. Father Coleman emphasized that Catholic education, which has been lagging in this area, must have a much broader approach. It must inform students about the opportunities available for the missionary work of the Church by becoming a member of a missionary order. But it also ought to discuss service as a lay person, working with clergy in overseas work or in government programs such as the Peace Corps. The whole concept of service to the community in the international sphere is new in Catholic education.

This idea is not new to the Protestant churches. It

is interesting to research the history of many of the leading people in the State Department and foreign service. Many are graduates initially of a Presbyterian college in the South which had a strong program of motivating people for international service, not as missionaries necessarily, but as lay people. Many of the people who are leaders in our State Department today had missionary parents who were not clergymen in many cases but doctors, accountants, or sociologists.

If we study the missionary activities of the Methodist Board of Missions we find that they have been sending people overseas for years in various professions to work side by side with clergy in various projects. From the standpoint of the Catholic Church this whole issue of service to the community must be presented to our young people as a much broader variety of opportunities. Catholic education has a responsibility and an opportunity. It should still have the missionary with his recruiting films. But it must bring other opportunities to the attention of the children. Today one can be a dedicated Christian serving God and fellow men in a wide variety of ways as compared to the one idea in the past that service could only be rendered as a priest, nun, or missionary.

Today the great issues in society are going to be served and settled by governments rather than ecclesiastical institutions. Christians can exert pressure from without as voters and from within as servants. The problems and opportunities for a person working within governmental structures for Christian service are many. The Church must help fulfill this vocation.

MOTIVATION

The most difficult problem from the pragmatic standpoint is motivation. It is difficult for a government to provide the motivation for the human action and human perfection fundamental to self-development and self-fulfillment. This is a concept fundamentally theological and spiritual; a component that the government is not in a position to supply. Some of the difficult assignments in these programs require a tremendous amount of Christian dedication which can only come from a spiritual and moral commitment. A government official, civil servant, or staff member may have problems of conscience as to whether or not a particular government policy or its implementation conforms to Christian principles. This is one of the dilemmas that many people in government service who are religious have.

The government is a secular organization and it cannot have the same requirements for moral and spiritual commitment as the Church for persons in charge of programs. When a church or ecclesiastical organization, whether it be a religious order or a congregation, calls a person to service and accepts him, it has standards of spiritual and moral excellence as well as of professional competence. Formerly all that was necessary was to be a holy, pious, good person, a state in which one could do anything for the Church. Today one has to have professional competence and skill for Church service.

In the government there is a priority placed on "excellence." Excellence in human personality, however, includes spiritual and moral qualities. Yet when the government selects people and evaluates their competence, it cannot take into account their moral and spiritual qualities. This is a limitation on the effectiveness of government in the problem of trying to work in the most basic areas of human and moral development.

The government now has large responsibilities in the fields of health, education, and welfare, which were historically the province of the churches. There is a resultant problem of the almost total absence or irrelevance of religion in these areas today. This need not be a critical factor. On the other hand it does give pause to many people.

RELEVANCE OF RELIGION

The teacher in the Harlem school, for instance, faces children who are completely devoid of cultural resources and of any spiritual or moral training in their homes. Working with these children one soon realizes that the children need a large dose of moral and spiritual formation as well as intellectual and physical development in the total educational process. Otherwise we cannot help them achieve the human development they need. This is a difficult challenge to people working in the educational area. There is therefore a dual role for both ecclesiastical and secular establishments in solving the problems of health, education, and welfare that our people have, that our nation has, and that other nations have.

Individual persons in government have staggering

responsibilities involving enormous sums of money and the welfare of millions of people. They have a need for ecclesiastical guidance and often they recognize this.

There are many people who feel that the Church and organized religion are irrelevant to the problems of modern society. On the other hand there are those in churches and religious organizations who have not recognized or are not aware that many programs for human betterment are really the province of the government.

The National Institute of Mental Health reports that the principal case-finding source for mental-health institutions are clergymen. More mentally ill people (40 per cent) are initially detected by clergy than by any other contact. In achieving the objective of mental-health programs the role of the spiritual is exceedingly important. Research has strengthened this conviction and the Institute continues to work very closely with the clergy to develop a better program of mental health for the nation. The Institute maintains a close working relationship with individual clergymen to achieve the goal of mental health for all American citizens. This is a very specific kind of relationship.

The Public Health Service makes grants for research in health problems to all types of agencies, individuals, clinics, hospitals, medical schools, and individual researchers. The people in the government health field recognize that historically the pioneers in health services have been the churches and religious orders. In this country 70 per cent of all health services are still provided by the private sector as contrasted to education, where about 70 per cent of education services are in the public sector. The largest proportion of research grants in the health field go to private organizations, institutions, hospitals, and clinics.

EDUCATION

This area of religion and education is one of the most controversial areas. We are in a period of great educational flux in this country and many people recognize that if we are going to give a complete education to a child we must include education in religious and theological matters as well as secular matters. This is now recognized in the area of higher education, but not on elementary and secondary levels where it is most crucial from an educational and psychological standpoint. The Federal Government and Congress recognize that in new programs of federal aid to education the children who are enrolled in Church-related schools as well as children who are enrolled in public schools have a right to federal aid. There is a recognition on the part of many people in government that religious education is an important part of education. This cannot be directly supported and subsidized by tax funds. In terms of achieving a high-quality educational program for all American youth the role of the churches must be recognized by the government. They have an important, essential contribution to make. This is a very concrete area in which we are feeling our way as a pluralistic society and trying to work out a new concept, a new approach. This has very important implications for overseas educational programs as well. The relationship between Peace Corps projects, for example, and the Church are often most intimately interdependent. The government cannot achieve the objectives of Peace Corps projects in many countries without intimate and cordial collaboration with the churches.

There is a shortage of priests not only in America but in missionary countries and therefore we are going to have to depend more and more upon the laity. How are we going to get more of the laity into this field? Can we look to our many Catholic colleges? Are Catholic graduates participating in proportion to their numbers and are they participating in proportion to the education they have received? Some think not.

In many missionary countries most of the education has been in the hands of the Church. Most of the men who are in positions of influence and power in these countries were students in Christian schools. Often we must question whether they are exerting the Christian influence that they have gained through their training. *De Ecclesia* reads: "Moreover, let the laity also by their combined efforts remedy the customs and conditions of the world, if they are an inducement to sin, so that they all may be conformed to the norms of justice and may favor the practice of virtue rather than hinder it" (No. 36).

CIVIL RIGHTS

This quotation applies further to the conditions that exist in our own southland. There is no doubt that the major spiritual, theological, and moral crisis of our society is the race problem. It has had a perverting effect upon the Church. It goes to the heart of the most fundamental of Christian virtues, the virtue of charity. It undermines it. Many concerned laymen in the South decided that the Church was not doing enough and that the only way to root out racism and do away with segregation and discrimination was through political action in the political order, utilizing the agencies of the government, the courts, and the Congress. Many Christian laymen in various denominations gave up trying to work through the Church to get at the basic sin which was segregation and racial discrimination. It is a commentary on our churches that they could not through their own moral fervor and strength accomplish this integration but had to seek the support of the government in righting a moral wrong. The Church and the state trod a parallel path.

There are thousands of young people flocking to noble causes through nonecclesiastical programs. They march out to remote lands in the Peace Corps or go down to the backwoods of Mississippi or Alabama or Georgia from our northern cities. They are attracted by poverty and affronted by the affluence of established societies and churches. They are not interested in building monuments or cathedrals but in working with people. They seek close contact with people who are poor and in trouble. Provide them with this and you can recruit them by the hundreds.

In Washington at Georgetown University, four hundred boys from the richest Catholic families in the United States are working in the slums three hours each day. In another Georgetown program thirty or forty students go down to Mexico to work with the

Indians in the most deprived villages of the backward provinces of Mexico. They pay their own transportation. If we offer such a challenge we can recruit many young men and women. This is a new challenge for Catholic educators: to channel young people into government programs, public welfare departments, public health clinics, settlement houses, and the like. The response is there waiting.

We have developed a theology of the priesthood, but not a theology of the laity. Today we are beginning to talk of the theology of the laity. We do not mean only that we want commentators and readers at Mass. We have to go beyond this. We have to answer the question: How can I be a good salesman or scientist, and still be a good Christian? Most people feel that if they are good Christians it is in spite of these activities. What we need to develop, theoretically as well as practically, is a clear view of how we can be good Christians because of these careers.

Wherever the laymen are, there is the Church, the Body of Christ. If we accept the definition of the Church as the people of God then the Church is in the government through its members. This is the modern apostolate.

Criteria for Programs in the Apostolate

DEWEY HEISING

American laymen, as taxpayers, as government and foundation officials, and as members of the lay apostolate, may admittedly have a responsibility to support programs which help developing countries. However, results to date show that these programs can be much improved, and a great deal of that improvement should take place at the grass roots of developing countries.

It is exactly at the grass roots that the missionaries are so effective. By applying some additional planning and management criteria to his many self-help projects and community activities, the missionary may well become the originator of better programs, worthy of increased United States voluntary, foundation, and governmental support.

SOCIAL APOSTOLATE

The shortage of local leaders in developing countries often throws missionaries into unusual situations. In Latin America, the directors of credit union federations in two countries are missionaries. In another country a priest operates a nationwide chain of radio stations which sponsor literacy programs. In Chile and Peru missionaries started the first savings and loan associations. Union movements in Colombia and Northeast Brazil owe their origins to priests.

The missionary is asked to be a leader, an organizer, and an educator. He tries to help his parishioners grow bigger crops. He helps them obtain credit to purchase needed tools, and he looks for a means whereby the chronically unemployed may gain employment. When visiting in the United States, the missionary may seek further assistance for his work, such as used equipment for a vocational training school. His friends give funds to purchase hybrid seeds and fertilizer for a demonstration farm, and he himself may approach a foundation or government agency for items such as a pump and diesel motor so a village can have water.

Because of his education, the missionary often sees the needs of communities more readily than their inhabitants do. Moreover, he holds the confidence of the people. As a result, he may volunteer to direct a community development or other self-help program, such as those mentioned above. These are hardly activities for which he was trained and they sometimes mean new problems which can grow into enormous complexities for him.

The problems can be partially avoided and the complexities reduced by some hard and factual thinking when he begins an enterprise. At that point, the missionary may want some expert advice.

PROFESSIONAL ASSISTANCE

At the Institute for Human Progress, private groups and voluntary agencies receive advice on the preparation and presentation of grant and loan applications to agencies under the Alliance for Progress. Almost without exception, we must ask each applicant agency to clarify its own objectives in order to see how they compare with those of the agency from which funds are requested. Almost always the objectives are basically similar but may require a change of emphasis, or just an understanding of how one's own program fits into the global picture. With objectives identical to the resource agency the applicant is no longer seeking a handout, but has raised himself to the level of a respected partner who contributes toward meeting the country's chief needs, and whose program merits consideration for expansion.

Determining the most desirable method for implementing and financing a project is as important as identifying its objectives.

A remarkable bishop from a South American country obtained funds abroad to establish several developmental services in his diocese, notably a radio education program, and a combination rural training center and demonstration farm. The farm was not producing as much income as anticipated and the diocese found it difficult to maintain the operating cost of the services. With the assistance of a research institute, the bishop formed a plan for a land-reform education program on a contract basis with the government agrarian reform agency. In effect, the same developmental services will now be given on a reimbursable basis.

A Jesuit priest in Mexico sought advice from a U.S. vocational training technician before he set up his school. He was advised to make a manpower survey among prospective employers to determine present and future needs in the community for skilled workers; also he was urged to seek an advisory committee of businessmen to plan and support the program. This is far different from constructing a building, ordering equipment, and then wondering what can be done with it.

As a footnote, the Jesuit received not only advice, but also six machine lathes for his school.

Planning and managerial expertise in the past has been largely limited to needs of United States and European business firms. More recently, U.S. management consultants have been employed by beneficiary governments receiving large United States development loans. Today, this expertise is available within most countries.

A potential source of planning experts whose services might be made available to private projects on a limited basis is the national planning or development agency of the host government. Then, the Agency for International Development Mission at the U.S. Embassy usually has a staff of experts in several fields of activities, such as education, agriculture, cooperatives, etc.

The universities in the host country are an excellent source of planning assistance, especially their economics faculties. Private development and research institutes are appearing now in many countries. Mention must be made of the International Federation of Institutes for Social and Socio-religious Research with headquarters in Brussels, Belgium. The Federation has member institutes in 18 countries and affiliation with similar development institutes in many others. It is especially geared to attend to the planning needs of the missionary.

Among other things, an expert planner will help identify those objectives of a project which are important for success and for obtaining needed resources. The planner will also assign priorities and make recommendations on the use of scarce funds. Finally, he will help measure the progress attained.

Small self-help activities at the village and grassroots level may not require the full treatment from the expert planner. Nonetheless he should be consulted on whatever project is contemplated.

The cost of planning and management assistance varies greatly. Some businesses may pay $150 a day for a management expert. Yet many governmental and U.S. Agency for International Development advisors are willing to give some of their time just for the asking. Professional consultants with private institutions must receive some compensation. University professors are often available for part-time work. When assistance is sought from within the host country, the cost is usually much less.

To achieve success with community development projects, the intelligent use of a great deal of factual information is required. With the scarcity of resources in developing countries, it behooves everyone to seek expert advice before investing funds and materials in any activity.

Simply doing good can no longer be an acceptable criterion, either for project activity, or for giving funds. Before he supports a foreign aid project, or even a lay apostolate activity, the American layman, whether he is a government official, a foundation executive, or a lay volunteer, should ask for a meaningful and expertly constructed program. It should reflect a well-thought-out plan.

The Apostolate and the World

Elizabeth Reid

The basic stress in the Constitution on the Church is on the essential unity of the Christian vocation. The unity of the whole Christian vocation brings out the positive meaning of the lay role. The layman is a Christian, a member of Christ's holy nation, sharing in the priestly, prophetic, and kingly function of Christ, commissioned by the Lord Himself—not by the bishops or priests—to take part in the saving mission of the whole Church to the whole world.

How do we implement this new understanding of who we are, this new understanding of the layman in the Church. First, I think that up to now we have not fulfilled our specific vocation in any marked degree. I quote from the Constitution: "The laity, by their very vocation, seek the kingdom of God by engaging in temporal affairs and by ordering them according to the plan of God" (*De Ecclesia,* No. 31). The operative words are "engaging" and "ordering." To engage in temporal affairs is evident and we all have ideas of how we can do that. Ordering them according to God's plan is something more difficult. We are on very treacherous ground here. We must have a real understanding of the world and the Church in the world and the world in the Church, and of how the Church affects the world and the world affects the Church. Therefore the need is to have a sure attitude of mind in working within the secular structure.

CHURCH STRUCTURES

Until now lay persons in the Church in overseas mission involvement worked within Church structures. Any layman who engaged in temporal affairs was not seriously considered as involved in the mission of the Church. In order to meet this new understanding I suggest that those of us who work in the world community make a concerted effort to become engaged in temporal affairs, especially in those parts of the world where there is very meager, very little Christian presence. I think first of the continent of Asia. Then I think of the Middle East. Then I think of some parts of Africa. I say this even to the point that some of us should move out of Church-related structures and go out into the world and witness with our person and our professional competency, without any props or buildings or the strength gained from small Christian strongholds in the midst of a pluralistic society. Persons engaged in this form of presence need to have an insight into the history of the apostolate. There needs to be an awareness that our work is part of a pattern. I refer again to the words of the Constitution, "ordering them according to the plan of God." Perhaps this definition of history might help us: "History is like a river poured forth from the mighty hand of God. It carries much cargo: the centuries, and the people. It flows toward the sea where the risen Christ awaits."

HISTORY

History, which is bound up in the continuing work of Christ down through the centuries, is the reason for the Church's being and the pattern of Her mysterious mission as Christ is made incarnate in society. I have come to understand this rather more clearly and acutely during my work for the typical missions of Palestine and the Catholic Near East Welfare Association. I have been traveling in Jordan, Syria, Lebanon, Egypt, and South India. I have walked along the way of conquerors and crusaders, of the great armies of Alexander and the Babylonian invaders. I have walked where the Philistine warriors came and the Egyptian armies, and where hosts of British and French and Australian and American fighting men have trod. I could not but be aware of the unbroken succession of generations of men. At the same time I had the recurring sensation of the fact that in this stretch of earth three of the world's greatest religions were born, Judaism, Christianity, and Islam. Each has a continuing faith in the human person, each has values and precepts and a will for peace. And yet, in this history-laden place, there is no peace. Injustice and lies and hatred and tyranny continue.

All generations crest in the two great events which dominate our time. I refer to the awakening of the Church to the realization that it is the people of God, and to the awakening of the masses to a sense of human dignity. These two great events are meant in God's plan to meet and fertilize each other. This concurrence defines precisely the presence of the Church in the world today and poses three presumptions. First, it means that we are becoming aware that Christianity is a Gospel which not only announces good tidings but brings them to the world in concrete form. It makes things new, redeems the time, brings about a more fully human development of life, brings about situations which are a little more redeemed. It answers the yearning and the cries of the masses for full human development. Second, it emphasizes the religious and apostolic importance of the lay life in all its diverse manifestations, as a manifestation of the lay vocation in secular structures. Thirdly, it stresses the importance of dialogue with its double dimension of tension and response. Tension is first. From the tension comes the response. This is something we white Westerners have not learned to do: to listen and to have a stimulus and response going on between person and person.

The awakening of the masses of people in the new nations and their entrance into the historical scene is more than an economic, political, or international event. It is also a spiritual and moral event. It has to do with the birth of a new humanity, with greater solidarity and more awareness of collective responsibility. I think this is a very important point.

We are witnessing a new humanism in which man is defined by responsibility. The construction of a more human world is a work which is not only economic but also moral and thus concerns the Christian as much as anyone else. *Pacem in Terris* and the Constitution on the

Church in the Modern World say these things in a different way. These documents suppose a high moral quality, with great justice and tenderness. They demand that an understanding of the new humanism bring with it a greater awareness of collective responsibility.

This is the layman's purpose.

A Catalogue of Needs

PETER KIMM

Implementing lay responsibility requires an investigation of specific suggestions for the laity on the question of the distribution of wealth. In Latin America, with a population roughly equal to that of the United States and Canada, the people have about one-eighth of our income. It is less effectively distributed than income in this half of the hemisphere. Annual per-capita income runs from $7 in Haiti to slightly under $700 in Argentina, with an average of a little over $300. In the United States per-capita income approaches $3,000. A typical United States family eats nourishing food, watches its weight, and worries about financing a second or third car, while a situation of continuing poverty prevails in the Latin countries. Have not the United States and Western Europe, the Christian world, if you will, become the oligarchy of the world, living on an island of luxury surrounded by an ocean of poverty? The description that many of us like to attribute to the oligarchies in Latin America as the defenders of vested interests, also describes us.

FOREIGN AID

The first, broad, political, and main vehicle for the transfer of wealth from one nation to another at the present time is foreign aid. At the beginning of the Marshall Plan the United States put two per cent of its gross national product into foreign aid. It has steadily decreased the proportion since then, so that the bill recently passed by Congress represents less than one-half of one per cent of our gross national product. This reduction, as far as I know, has not been dictated by any improvements in the existing world situation. Rather the world situation gets worse and worse and disparity in wealth becomes worse. Yet the Congress does not believe that the people of the United States want a stronger foreign-aid program. Politicians react to what they believe to be public opinion.

I would like to present some testimony given recently before Congress:

> We believe, we firmly believe that the United States can and should spend at least one per cent of its total national output for aid to the developing countries. Yet the authorizations in the bill before you equal less than half that amount. The one per cent sum would be 6.6 billion a year. The current bill allows for 3.2 billion. Our gross national product has increased by more than 20 per cent since 1960. Our nation is wealthier by more than one-fifth. Yet as a proportion of that wealth our effort in support of foreign aid has been growing constantly smaller. We believe this to be a great wrong. We urge the Congress and the Administration to reverse that trend.

Inevitably because of this bill some of our wealth will be transferred overseas to help the poor and hungry. To that extent only will it adversely affect our balance of payments and then only temporarily. To the critics that say that this cannot continue on indefinitely we say it can. Our wealth is in our farms and in our factories. In our minds and in our skills. We can give away a portion of the wealth we create each year, and we can give it away indefinitely. Only a miser could contend that the richest nation on earth should receive more than it gives.

CHURCH'S ATTITUDE

That testimony is not from any Catholic organization but from the AFL-CIO. It causes a question to be directed to the institutional Church and to the lay organizations in the Church. Where are your statements? Where is your pressure? Where is the pressure from Christians for some equitable distribution of wealth or some move in that direction?

The public generally accepts as a Church concern the flow of U.S. resources into underdeveloped countries through missionary organizations. Statistics are difficult to come by, because of the many-headed structure of Church aid. Approximately 13½ million dollars are disbursed to the missions from the United States through the Propagation of the Faith. Another 35 million is collected by the various religious orders, of which about 75 per cent is sent overseas. Possibly a million dollars goes to Latin America through the Latin America Bureau and the Near East Welfare Conference. Catholic Relief Services sends 25 million dollars.

An unmeasurable amount goes out through individual dioceses.

It is fair to state that if you add together all of these sums the total flow is less than 100 million dollars a year. This is about $10 a family per year for Catholic families. In relation to the amount of money that the Church in the United States is putting into the education of children this missionary amount is woefully small. Education is a worthy venture, but I cannot imagine any scale of values placing it on a higher plane than relieving poverty and misery for the people of the world.

I would like to see Catholic laymen and the institutional Church create pressure and take a public position of support of foreign aid. Secondly, I would like to see the bishops of the United States set up an annual collection or a series of collections similar to the Misereor and the Adveniat collections in Germany, and to a proposed program recently adopted by the Scottish bishops for support of overseas social and economic projects. Such a collection should easily raise another 100 million added to the current 100 million. We will have to spend a little less on something else, that is the problem. I would like to see a restructuring of Church policy to implement this attempt.

A Latin American cardinal claimed that one of his great problems is that he cannot borrow money except at very high interest rates. Many international organizations are providing money at low interest rates for governments and other programs but there is no program available for the bishops of Latin America to borrow at equitable rates. I see no reason why the bishops of the United States could not create a committee to use their high credit ratings with a guarantee of repayment of loans to enable Latin American bishops to borrow at commercial rates in the United States.

These are areas of the apostolate—encouraging foreign aid, devising plans for assisting overseas ecclesiastical leaders with funds, and being continually aware of the possibilities and potential needs of the world Church.

Developing Societies: Missionary Orientation Toward Education and Social Change

FRANCIS X. GANNON

As is apparent, education is a term and activity of many meanings. For the most part, of course, it implies two things: the formal instructional process through which our potentialities of character and intelligence are allowed room to unfold or deepen; and the daily, informal activities wherein we randomly discover the rights and responsibilities or the interests and attitudes we require to subsist with a semblance of purpose, personal dignity, and reasonable self-sufficiency in a community with others. Both senses, at least insofar as final objectives are concerned, seem to coalesce in Hannah Arendt's comment that:

> Education is the point at which we decide whether we love the world enough to assume responsibility for it and by the same token save it from that ruin which, except for renewal, except for the coming of the new and young, would be inevitable. And education, too, is where we decide whether we love our children enough not to expel them from our world and leave them to their own devices, nor to strike from their hands their chance of undertaking some-

> thing new, something unforeseen by us, but to prepare them in advance for the task of renewing a common world.[1]

Education, in other words, could be described as the quest, the activity, or the training, whereby the individual discovers his capacities and limits, comes to understand his society and its goals, and prepares himself for cooperating with others in renewing the "common world."

A definition of this kind, however tentative, would probably not be acceptable in many quarters. Its irrelevancy would appear to those who hope to reduce education to a pure technical process in which, for example, teaching style would have priority over educational content. To this viewpoint the definition would not fit the educational dilemmas facing modern, industrialized societies, in which, many contend, education's purpose must in essence be technical not social—retraining individuals to survive constant technological obsolescence. The definition might also be disowned by those concerned only with higher education. This, as Newman observed, consists in the "cultivation of the intellect," not necessarily in laying the foundations for a practical renewal of the "common world." It could also be faulted by other groups, since it does not explicitly emphasize at least the constant Christian preoccupation that education is not only a preparation for our temporal existence, but more importantly, for eternity.

[1] Hannah Arendt, *Between Past and Future* (Meridian Books, Cleveland, World Publishing, 1961), p. 196.

EDUCATION IN UNDERDEVELOPED AREAS

Still, one can propose that while the definition does not extend to all horizons about the nature of education, it does reflect what education is and must be today in unevenly developed countries like those in Latin America and in underdeveloped societies, as in Asia and Africa. For there education surely cannot be limited to the narrow concepts of professional educators, nor become simply a technical training process. On the contrary, in these countries it involves a host of formal or informal activities or training programs through which individuals and groups must be prepared for their uncharted responsibilities in shaping their common world. This means that not only must education be adapted to the uniquely contemporary tasks of social renewal in these regions, but it must also make its contribution in such a way as to help build cohesive communities and provide an identity of national and social purpose for these societies.

This is at best an overpowering assignment for education, but one which political circumstances today seem to call for. In *Which Way Africa?*, Basil Davidson highlights some of the problems underlying the challenge of forming individuals who will be able to work at building a "common world" for Africa's newly emerged countries.

> How is it going to be possible, for example, to spend money on agricultural development—the necessary ground for every advance in this continent now—unless farmers and peasants can be carried into intelli-

> gent participation? The mere distribution of tractors, fertilizers, instructors and the like will accomplish little but waste and disillusion unless these new instruments are used to refashion the traditional system and they cannot be so used without their actual acceptance by country folk who are still embedded in traditional ways of thought. Such active acceptance of the need for far reaching change depends on wedding the cause of political independence to the cause of social and economic reconstruction, and the same may be said of the multiplication of schools and universities, or the founding of new industries. Their fruitfulness will depend on the creation of a political expansion—in Africa today, to rapid and deliberate social change; and this in turn can only be the product of a massive activation of democracy.[2]

To augment Mr. Davidson's views, let us recognize that the "massive activation" of the majority of the populations will, in general, accompany their direct involvement in social and political renewal. In contemporary Africa, for example, this would seem to mean that it becomes education's task to prepare the ground for this involvement, to contribute toward and to lay the foundations for the process of "rapid and deliberate social change," which alone can make the work of broad-based renewal possible. Education's contribution could be made in a variety of ways, and one must add, only circumstances, not abstract educational theories or distinctions—however essential they are in formulating approaches to social change—will be able to determine

[2] Basil Davidson, *Which Way Africa?* (Baltimore, Penguin Books, 1964).

the suitability and adequacy of educational programs. And only as education is in a position to make this contribution, only as it helps to stimulate individuals to participate in community action, to encourage widespread measures for social change, will it perhaps be in a position to fulfill the bewildering array of challenges extended to it by the African societies.

The same premises and objectives, no doubt in a markedly different manner, are applicable to Latin America. Differences in the application of these follow, since these global regions differ in history, economic structures, cultural traditions, and political institutions. Beyond this obvious fact, moreover, the differences are greater than they first seem, since in reality there is not one but two Latin Americas: the five or six larger industrial countries and the gradually urbanizing centers in even the smaller societies; and the Latin America of the rural zones. In these latter areas, where 6 per cent of the landholders own 75 per cent of the tillable land, approximately 75 per cent of the hemisphere's 200 million inhabitants subsist on the periphery of social existence, or as former President Romulo Betancourt once said, on the margin of "national life."

URBAN EDUCATION

Let us look at urban Latin America to exemplify the problems. Here the primary educational obstacles impeding the goals of social reordering or deflecting to the task of common renewal, must be viewed in order of priority from two aspects—first that of formal systematic education; and second that of community action. At the former level the overcoming of barriers includes guaranteeing that, in contrast to the past, educational structures and institutions, whether public or private, become instruments to foster social change and to open up equality of opportunity for all citizens.

To turn to the area of community action, it appears that where the initiation or expansion of urban community activities are concerned, the role of education is to relate itself to the dilemma of how to create new, or strengthen older but ill-formed, private organizations and intermediate social institutions. This could include forming leaders to help develop such institutions as trade unions, cooperatives, management societies or even, looked at as social communities, parishes which traditionally in Latin America, despite large numbers of Christians and a host of ecclesiastical edifices, have been few and far between. In addition, at this level education could well be related to a little-noticed but critical task, the task of helping to clarify and distinguish the unoriginal but clashing social ideologies which permeate the hemispheric mentality and help frustrate the growth of understanding among diverse social sectors.

RURAL EDUCATION

In all global regions a reversal of educational priorities seems required outside the urban complex, as in the rural zones today community awakening rather than formal schooling has paramount importance. Here the major educational questions, in consequence, include how to activate communities, provide groups with a sense of mission and purpose, and form emerging leaders. With respect to the latter, training should be so designed as to equip these leaders to manage social change not for their own self-interest but for the immediate tasks of common renewal. As assistance for efforts of this kind an armoury of well-tested instruments is available for gaining practical experience in community action—credit unions, farmers clubs, radio schools, literacy and agricultural programs.

To a significant degree the democratic awakening of these rural populations, reflected in attempts to engage them in common tasks aimed at improving their welfare, cannot and will not wait until formal educational systems are functioning everywhere in rural zones, and in another generation or two may be fully underway on a national scale at least in all Latin American countries. But even this change does not preclude the parallel and indeed insistent need here and now for education to contribute to extensive increases in community activities. The harsh reality for the majority of rural dwellers in most global regions, now and for the foreseeable future living without the security which comes from formal education or technical training, is that they exist in a state of social disarray and disorganization. In 1962 the Chilean Bishops focused on this situation in a well-known pastoral letter whose strictures are applicable everywhere. Great numbers of illiterate and mainly rural citizens are, they pointed out, "left to solve their problems by simple intuition, left to the dictates of common sense which reality contradicts, to an innocent confidence which rapidly vanishes before a hostile world . . . [they] must face a legal order which they do not understand, and the justice of which is not so attainable to them as it is for other members of our society."

CHALLENGES CREATED BY MODERN COMMUNICATION

It is this state of affairs which cannot long survive—and indeed is turning upside down everywhere, although some question whether change is coming with sufficient speed to preclude social cataclysm in many societies. It is not that rural material and social well-being in many global regions will be improved sharply overnight, although perhaps unrelated dramatic improvements are possible. No, the point is that with the introduction of modern communications systems, and the opening up of penetration and feeder roads, even the most remote area is no longer inaccessible to the contemporary world, to its attendant pressures for social change and personal mobility. Affected by this process the once dormant rural poor, now aware of the modern world, are pressing toward some organized stake in this change. How to channel these demands, to give some concrete realization to popular aspirations, to spur community leadership and efforts toward integrating the rural poor into their own societies, are among the essential contemporary educational challenges. These challenges, moreover, have not yet been seriously faced under government-to-government aid programs like the Alliance for Progress in Latin America, a situation evidenced by the lack of popular participation in and enthusiasm for this and similar ventures. Nor, it seems advisable to stress, can these challenges be met adequately, at least so far as one now foresees, by merely seeking to provide elementary or primary education to all, especially since this objective, in any event, is currently itself a still distant alternative in nearly all parts of the world.

Today, it is a truism to say that the response of anyone working in the field of education to the quest for common renewal in Asia, Africa, and South America, if it is to be seriously related to actual human needs, must be tentative and many-sided, sensitively alert to local conditions and requirements.

To be effective, moreover, it is recognized that such a response must at least look beyond traditional approaches to social action in these regions which, however valuable for their time and place, consisted in emphasizing the development of formal primary schooling or other tested social institutions. Today with the intense clamor for social change, while situations may call for schools to be built, they also may not; rather the need may be for assistance to help create new social institutions or to reinfuse into old ones, e.g., public universities, a sense of Christian humanism.

COOPERATION WITH NATIONAL AGENCIES

There will be difficulties involved in taking this approach, in re-evaluating whether one's efforts really face up to contemporary educational and community needs. Some will find it hard, even with the best intentions, to determine which direction to take. One possible source of help in making such a determination could be the national social and economic development plans now being drawn up in many countries. By relating its own efforts to these national plans, provided they are realistic and properly formed, the missionary response might receive some guidelines for its own objectives, notably so where education is concerned.

To a considerable degree, one cannot fail to recognize that this newer framework and direction for missionary social and educational action could lead this to become attuned more toward primarily temporal rather than directly ecclesial activities. Thus, efforts would be tilted toward setting up credit unions and cooperatives, running agricultural or other leadership training programs and working within the environment of some national university systems.

To note that the emphasis in the social and educational field may be directly temporal is not, let us not overlook, to say that even in such activities spiritual formation is therefore to be cast aside or neglected. *Pacem in Terris,* consistent with the traditions of the social encyclicals, advises otherwise, underscoring that in all kinds of temporal activities, education must be integral. In the words of John XXIII, "It is indispensable that in the training of youth, education should be complete and without interruption, namely that religious values should be cultivated and the moral conscience refined in a manner to keep pace with the continuous and ever more abundant assimilation of scientific and technical knowledge." [3] To paraphrase: an increase in technical information about a coopera-

[3] John XXIII, "Peace on Earth," Our Sunday Visitor edition, p. 49.

tive does not necessarily lead to better community or personal living.

Yet even when we place this caveat at the forefront of our vision, the contrary is equally true. Namely, as the Constitution on the Church insists, no one can forget that "the temporal sphere is governed by its own principles, since it is rightly concerned with the interests of this world" (*De Ecclesia*, No. 36). As a result, prior to entering into parallel or joint efforts within this sphere, or prior to placing itself at the service of contemporary man's common quest for social renewal, the missionary church, just like any other entity, must understand the principles behind the modernizing temporal institutions with which it intends to work. As this is done, as an adequate comprehension is gained of these institutions and their purpose and nature, the missionary response may well learn how to cooperate in renewing or establishing programs with these, not as adjuncts to ecclesial endeavors, but as socially valuable and relatively autonomous activities for their own sake. Once cooperative action proceeds on this plane, it no longer becomes simply a matter of doing one more good work, but of relating one's educational and social action programs to the fullest needs of developing or emerging communities—as these are seen by the communities themselves.

A WORK FOR THE LAITY

In the long run and wherever possible even now, these temporal but missionary-assisted social and educational activities will be the preoccupation of the laity.

This is the case since, as *De Ecclesia* stresses, in the work of permeating the temporal creation with the spirit of Christ so that "it may more effectively fulfill its purpose in justice, charity, and peace," "the laity have the principal role" (No. 36).

No one should overlook, on the other hand, that at the present time and even for the foreseeable future in Africa, Asia, and Latin America, noticeably so in the rural zones, this admonition will be more frequently a counsel of perfection than a realizable possibility. For, the reality is that in most instances, as is evident by what has already been and is being accomplished in many regions and communities, the missionary initiatives in social and educational efforts come chiefly from the clergy. The plain fact is that, apart from an occasional and inadequate governmental or military presence, in particular in rural areas, the only visible, responsible, and trusted modernizing influence is often that of the missionary clergy. On its shoulders, therefore, must fall the heavy, immediate burdens of making effective the missionary response to the universal challenges posed by the demands for social change.

That this must be the case now does not of course negate the fundamental premise—the work of reconstructing the temporal order is principally the work of the laity. Since this is so, it appears correct for the missionary clergy to recognize that while circumstances now call them to new arenas of social action, their long-range aim and even interests must be to withdraw from these spheres or at least to re-evaluate their own roles with respect to this sphere as they bring the laity into their own.

Depending on the situations and countries, responses to the educational needs of developing communities must be highly flexible. Yet recognizing this we can propose a "catalogue of needs" for educational priorities, a catalogue applicable to all regions of the globe and to which the missionary church, because of its unique abilities, can most significantly respond. While the following list is drawn up with Latin America in mind, I would suggest that primary world-wide educational priorities include:

1. The development of global campaigns to eliminate illiteracy.
2. The formation of leaders for social action and the provision of assistance to these leaders to help them in the work of creating new social institutions, or, as some prefer to call these, community organizations.
3. The expansion of agricultural or other leadership training activities in rural areas.
4. Cooperation between the missionary church and the public university systems, especially in the areas of philosophy or social thought.
5. Within the United States the creation of education, orientation, and action centers designed to support overseas missionary operations.

ILLITERACY

The framework for the first measure—participation in a world-wide attack on illiteracy—was set by President Lyndon B. Johnson in September 1965 at the bicentennial celebration of the Smithsonian Institution.

According to the President, "Today, more than 700 million adults . . . dwell in darkness where they cannot read or write . . . and unless the world can find a way to extend the light, the forces of that darkness may ultimately engulf us all." To help preclude such from coming to pass, the President indicated that "This Government and this Nation is prepared to join in finding a way," and that he was establishing a task force to determine how the U.S. might contribute to supporting this objective. The President also signified his intention "to call on leaders in both public and private enterprise to join with us in mapping this effort."

Is there not in the President's message a clear call to all men of good will involved in the world-wide work of common renewal, a challenge applicable in particular to those who daily stand in the front lines of this work? And is it not impossible for this challenge to be met decisively if responsible groups everywhere do not seriously respond to it? How, for example, can the campaign even get underway in some Latin American countries, where 40 per cent of all children attending school are already in the parochial system, if this system is not put at the service of world-wide campaigns to uproot illiteracy, if it does not engage in special efforts to run educational programs on something more than a 9:00 A.M. to 3:00 P.M. schedule? And is not this question even more pertinent in other regions, where the educational plant or services of the parochial system is 60 to 70 per cent of the existing and projected national total?

Obviously, the answer is that if proposals like this are to become anything more than mirages, all resources, private and public, must be put to work at once. Two immediate steps might be taken to evidence the willingness and readiness of the missionary church to collaborate in this effort. First, the U.S. mission-sending societies might indicate to President Johnson how their resources could support this projected world-wide endeavor to improve the educational levels of all men. Secondly, in Asia, Africa, and Latin America an inventory might be taken of missionary or parochial resources, human and technical, available to assist the proposal to become more than an aspiration.

There are some valid objections to permitting full participation by the missionary and parochial systems in an endeavor of this kind. Some objections, however, especially those that rest on fears about the inherent dangers arising from cooperation between Church and state, have already been largely answered within our own society. Recognizing, for example, that "the war on poverty" and help to disadvantaged children are everybody's business or nobody's, we have initiated widespread programs of community and educational action, programs in which private and public efforts are fully blended. Examples of this type of cooperation are found in such programs as the 1965 Aid to Education Act, and Project Star, the $7 million training and redevelopment poverty program for Mississippi coordinated by the Catholic Diocese of Jackson-Natchez and Methodist and Baptist organizations. If we can successfully involve all groups in our society in what all agree is our task of common renewal, can we do less, particularly if we hope to succeed in our efforts, in those areas of the world where hunger and grinding poverty stalk entire communities?

LEADER FORMATION

The second specific educational matter in developing areas to which attention could be directed is the issue of the formation of leaders for emerging social institutions and the provision of technical assistance to these leaders and their institutions. Until quite recently little attention was paid to this area, but at the present time various organizations—one could cite the American Institute for Free Labor Development and the Credit Union International Association—are engaged heavily in Latin American programs of leadership formation for trade unions and cooperatives. It would seem, however, that more extensive activities of that nature are required, not directed toward training leaders to work within specific social organizations but orienting them to cooperate with each other in modernized groups or organizations of any kind. In societies where intermediate modern social institutions are conspicuously lacking but urgently required, the key problem is not that people do not know how to work together in specific organizations like trade unions, but that they simply have little experience in cooperating in any organized programs leading to rapid social change. Whether such managerial experience can be imparted solely through courses in leadership formation is, of course, debatable. What does not appear arguable, though, is that cadre information given to those who have already demonstrated leadership abilities can help them to become better equipped to direct organizational activities in a more effective manner. Both reason and experience attest to this point.

How to offer such leadership training is another question. An example which might be studied for guidelines is the program established for Central American youth leaders by Loyola University, New Orleans, Louisiana, through its Inter-American Institute. In cooperation with the Agency for International Development, this Institute—in which five universities, Louisiana State, Tulane, Xavier, Dillard, and Loyola, have joined forces—conducts a two-month cadre seminar for a total of 180 young leaders each year. In brief, the program calls for training in social ideas and organizational techniques so that these 18- to 35-year-old leaders will gain a more thorough understanding of the nature, purpose, and organization of modern social institutions. The course does not prepare individuals to work in specific organizations. It does seek, however, to give them an awareness of the diverse kinds of social groupings their own societies may require to foster social change. It also affords them an understanding of how the goals of these different groups are interrelated.

The Inter-American Institute is aiming to carry this program forward by opening branches in Central America. At these branches training would then be offered to greater numbers of individuals with the original graduates of the program serving as instructors, and concrete "pilot project" activities would be undertaken within specific organizations to demonstrate the applicability of the insights obtained through classroom instruction.

Few would suggest that this kind of diffusive training is the sole answer to the community leadership-formation needs in emerging societies. But, at the very least, a venture of this kind represents an original approach to the difficult problem of providing community and organizational leaders with greater sensitivity to their own objectives and to the means of arriving at these. Other parties interested in encouraging the formation of young leaders for social development might, in consequence, take a look at this New Orleans project and perhaps evaluate their own intentions, work, and dilemmas in the light of its results.

RURAL AGRICULTURAL LEADERS

Another essential educational task is the formation of rural community and agricultural leaders. Despite contrary popular opinions, rural communities in developing areas often possess highly developed social systems, but these systems are too often not adapted to coping with the goals of modernization. In the face of the clamorous pressures for social change, this means that rural leaders require instruction in basic education and agricultural techniques and in community action.

On almost all sides the range of training called for includes instruction in irrigation, fertilizer uses, and seed techniques. Such training should be related to programs for general sanitation and health improvements, the development of cooperatives and credit unions, and instruction in general culture, handicraft industries, and agriculture.

In countless communities across the globe one or another of these training programs or activities has long been underway. What has been generally lacking, though, is the creation of well-planned centers in which training might be imparted to large numbers of rural leaders, and follow-up activities with them initiated in their home communities. Such centers, located in the rural zones, could run training sessions on a periodic basis and help establish local community centers in various key surrounding towns and villages. In this way a feedback process between the center and the local communities might perhaps be set in motion to ensure that trainees are realistically applying their knowledge. In addition, such centers, by serving as coordinating points could develop bonds between presently unrelated social projects, something which should give strength to the now diverse activities of many separate groups.

Who would establish these rural training centers and how is another issue itself. Certainly, however, support would be forthcoming from national or international agencies to any on-going facility which had already demonstrated its capabilities and its contribution to social development.

At best, orienting the missionary response to the newer task of "common renewal" will be difficult. Some old habits, attitudes, and activities must be discarded and a different manner of looking at social and educational reality envisioned, if this response is to be effective. The difficulties in making these adjustments are not insuperable but they must be seen as real ones.

RESTRUCTURING THE SOCIAL SYSTEM

For one thing, individuals and groups embarking on better planned and developmentally-oriented social and educational activities must first come to possess an awareness of what these newer directions entail for their vision and efforts. They must come to see that unlike as in the past, today's social efforts cannot consist simply in doing one more good work, but require looking at the issues involved in restructuring or rebuilding entire social systems, or at least making an effective contribution toward this goal. Otherwise, if this is not the basis on which participation in common renewal goes forward, the danger will be that countervailing social forces and tides, many of an antihuman nature, may simply engulf and destroy the solitary, isolated efforts, no matter how immediately constructive and socially beneficial, which are undertaken on a piecemeal basis. In effect, this would seem to imply that the Church must make constant efforts within each country to coordinate its own social and educational activities, to direct these toward fairly common national objectives, and to relate its own work to that of other private and public, religious or nonreligious endeavors, wherever this is possible.

MISSIONARY TRAINING

Secondly, adjustments to this approach in the field of education and social development should be reflected in the kinds of training, orientation, and support from their U.S. resources received by the missionary individuals and groups going into developing societies. At present, too many of these individuals arrive in a country ready and willing to become involved in the whirl of social development but inadequately aware of the limitations imposed by the environment and by their own capabilities, as well as by the low level of support they will receive from their U.S. or other base. On occasion these individuals then become the ones, who, as Louis and André Rétif have observed,

> have not been able to adapt themselves, who are a deadweight, a hindrance, whose presence does more harm than good. Yet through negligence, lack of authority or of courage, they are left where they are and no account is taken of their sometimes baneful influence. The times are too serious for such lacunae, inertia and obstacles to be tolerated.[4]

That this charge is a serious one, but possesses considerable validity, is an opinion shared by many concerned observers. And the situation can in large part be remedied, many agree, through proper training and orientation for those going overseas, provided, however, that adequate supporting assistance continues to be made available to them from their home base. Orientation by itself is not sufficient, for as the experience of groups like the Peace Corps and other voluntary organizations illustrates, the real problems arise when

[4] Louis and André Rétif, *op. cit.*, pp. 54-55.

one seeks to obtain the financial, material, or human assistance needed to get community and educational activities underway.

A MISSIONARY ASSISTANCE CENTER

What these thoughts lead up to, I would propose, is that a center or centers must be created in the United States to provide training and supporting assistance for North American missionaries going abroad. At present there exist several institutes in which formation programs are undertaken: for Latin America the better known include Cuernavaca, Mexico; Ponce, Puerto Rico; and the Agency for International Development, Patterson. Recently, moreover, CARA (The Center for Applied Research in the Apostolate) was established to serve as a coordinating U.S. institute for fostering basic studies and action programs for the church's educational, urban affairs, and community action programs. CARA will seek to develop action-oriented studies for the United States, as well as to serve as a coordinating point in the U.S. with similar research organizations in other countries. Its program should prove a boon to those who require information about what social action projects can or must be developed in specific societies and how to go about undertaking these projects.

But if the picture has brightness in the area of missionary orientation and applied research, the same is not so where the provision of supporting assistance is concerned. Once the missioner is prepared to initiate his program, he runs headlong into difficulties, since unless he is particularly fortunate or farsighted he must develop everything from scratch and on his own. What a contrast to international agencies like the Agency for International Development, which buttresses its overseas operations by Washington desk officers fully prepared to find the kinds of assistance required by overseas technicians. The contrast, moreover, often reduces itself to the missioner wasting endless hours seeking information, making contacts, and getting technical help to develop, for instance, a co-operative; when, if he were supported by a U.S. office his task would be enormously simplified and he would not, as happens too frequently, find himself repeating the errors and frustrations already experienced by countless predecessors.*

There have been some attempts to remedy this situation, to provide some kind of central U.S. supporting assistance to the missioners who see the urgent mandate to join in the tasks of common renewal. Yet, these efforts, few would doubt, are too sporadic, unrelated, and unambitious to be realistically effective. What seems to be required is the establishment of an organization like the Institute for Human Progress, magnified by about a thousand per cent. The IHP is a small privately-financed, Washington-based organization which offers technical assistance, especially to help develop projects for submission to international fund-granting agencies, and its services are at the disposal of any private sector group, including religious organiza-

* [Ed. Note: Many of the services required from such an assistance center, in the form of technical information for missioners, may be obtained from the Maryknoll Overseas Extension Service (MOES) by writing to Maryknoll, New York 10545.]

tions or institutions. The limitations of this Institute, for the kind of center envisioned here, are chiefly its small size and its emphasis on Latin America. The IHP's set-up could surely be studied, however, to determine the type of organizations which are most needed to provide U.S. supporting technical and, above all, financial aid to missionary activities in Africa, Asia, and South America. The Institute, in any case, is already doing in embryo what must be done on a vast scale, if the missionary contribution to world social renewal is not to become simply ineffective or perhaps altogether a chimera.